MOSAIC REPUBLIC

TIGER WORKU

Mosaic Republic

©2022 Tiger Worku

ISBN: 978-1-66783-674-4

Table of Contents

Chapter 1:

Twelve Years A Student

TEARS. WHEN I STARTED my first day of kindergarten, I used tears to express my emotions. Yes, I was that kid.

The reason I brought up that comical yet troubling memory is the same reason we want to listen to and understand other people's stories. What at first seems to be a simple moment in time subconsciously turns itself into a memory that we later look back on and ponder over. When or if we decide to share this memory with others, we unknowingly spark a fire that does one of two things (1) gradually sizzle down and maybe reignite only to sizzle down again as a pattern emerges (2) spread like a wildfire only to grow bigger than what any climate could contain. Through shared memories, we can feel anger, tranquility, jubilation, fear, sadness & motivation. Memories are imperative going forward because that's what I predicate this chapter on. As the ostensibly self-proclaimed connoisseur of the power of memories, I've got some that I think are worth sharing. The reason I'm sharing these memories specifically is that I believe in them lies answers to some of our most pressing issues in terms of our schooling system. Besides snowstorms and the term "you betcha" Minnesota is nationally known for some of the worst disparities in education among poor rural students, poor urban students, and students born with a silver spoon in their mouth — maybe those tears weren't so extraneous after all. As a student who went through the Minneapolis Public Schools system, I was exposed to a concoction of distinct personalities, cultures, genders & ideas; thus making me a vigorous proponent of public schools to this day. I was also exposed to a bitter truth that still lurks through our schools' hallways: Although diversity may seem as simple as a numbers game for some, in reality, it's a complex and transformative change that's analogous to destroying a building and rebuilding it with a new name. As a second-generation American whose parents immigrated to the United States from Ethiopia, the value of an excellent education and my duty to attain it were instilled in me at a young age. In a state like Minnesota where people who share the same complexion as me make up about 6.19%, you'd think being the only person with black skin in a room would largely compose my educational experience; and although that was the case sometimes, shockingly, I found myself to be in the majority more times than not. Besides Minneapolis, St. Paul, and some surrounding suburbs historically being the primary hub for people of color throughout the state. Newly emerging immigration patterns played an integral role not only in my experience but also in the experience of my peers, regardless of ethnicity or background. Because of wars in Laos and Somalia, massive waves of refugees flocked to the United States and made many states, including Minnesota, their new homes.

Preschool

IN PRESCHOOL, MY SISTER and I were the only two black kids, but by grade school; we were amongst the heterogeneous masses finding our way around the melting pot. My first cognizant experience with skin color dynamics was when our preschool took a trip to the local water park. What started as a fun day ended in disaster. Kids were itching and crying, teachers were applying ointment as fast as they could. Me? What was I doing? Well, I was too busy trying to place my tiny gluteus maximus on the water spout fountain. It was on the bus ride home I discovered the true strength of my melanin. Whenever precautions were put in place to put sunscreen on children before they left for subsequent field trips; I laughed in the face of the staff member lathering me in sunscreen and I laughed in the sun's face, too. My preschool years were filled with elation and proper development. There was that time where a substitute teacher confused my dietary restrictions (halal) with vegetarianism and wouldn't let me eat what was one of my favorite meals. I've since forgiven her. I was loved, and I loved everybody. During the year I graduated from preschool, my father passed away from Rhabdomyosarcoma, which is a rare but deadly form of cancer. I was so young, so the effect his death had on me from a conscious emotional standpoint was minimal. I remember hundreds of people visiting our house bringing whatever they could to help. Dr. Rank, my father's cancer doctor, showed up at my father's funeral and helped bury him as well. Dr. Rank befriended our family and has never stopped showing up from time to time to check in to this day. I often think about my father and the number of people he's touched, but I also think about how lucky he was to have the people he had in his life. I may not have been able to comprehend a lot, but I have never forgotten the faces of those who stepped up to help in whatever way they could.

Kindergarten

KINDERGARTEN WAS AN INTERESTING time for me. The local school (Seward Montessori) rejected my sister and me because of a lack of space. I later attended that school as described in the coming passages. As stated in the bold text at the beginning of the chapter, I cried my eyes out not only on the first day of school, but for the entire first week. It got so bad that the school arranged for me to meet with my older cousin, who was a couple of grades older than me, for mini counseling sessions. The teaching assistant made a little pamphlet for me and one other student, outlying how the day would go. The pamphlet helped pacify some of my anxiety, but nothing calmed me more than going outside. I don't know if it was the feeling of being trapped in or the idea of not being in control of my body, e.g., sitting criss-cross applesauce, standing in a line, staying silent for long periods. There was only one place I felt comfortable, and that was on the playground. During recess, I could engage with my peers without an inside voice. I could run as fast as I wanted for as long as I wanted; I had an amount of freedom that made me feel in control and, therefore, content. After getting through the first week of school, I quickly learned that I wasn't out of the woods yet. While some at the time viewed my display of sadness as a cute coming of age moment, others viewed it as a state of vulnerability that needed to be pounced on for self-conscious purposes. To a couple of my fellow kindergartners, I was an injured elk, and they were the pack of wolves ready to tear me apart. Luckily, my antlers were still in tack and what would have been a classic case of classroom bullying turned into an end-less bout of classroom warfare. I'll never forget when during a gym class one boy was making a face at me and I made one back. The gym teacher noticed, asked both of us to step forward on opposite sides of each other in front of the class, and proceeded with the words "If you two want to fight, then go ahead! Fight!" I remember staring at the teacher in disbelief. He put me at a massive disadvantage because I was significantly shorter, significantly weaker, and I didn't know how to fight. Until then, I relied on the staff to keep me from being physically harmed. My parents told me to run to a teacher if I was ever in said situation. I was afraid not only of being mauled by my insecure classmate but of also suffering a damaging blow to my reputation and my already intrinsically feeble self-esteem. As I looked at my classmate to gauge his feelings, it stunned me to see him with a wicked grin on his face accompanied by mini warm-up jumps ready to make his debut on what appeared to be the gym teacher's version of WWE. All I could think about was "how could an adult let this happen", I thought he would quickly intervene to get us to see the larger picture. I was sadly mistaken. As my peer made a blitz for me, I quickly dogged him and tried to run away. He chased after me and as he gained ground, I curled into the fetal position, determined to arch my back and tuck my head in like turtles often do as a defense mechanism. My classmate hovered over me, attempting to pick me up and roll me over. As I felt a manageable pressure, try to break my fortress, I screeched for help. I then felt the pressure slowly ease and the calming yet damming voice of my gym teacher say "that's enough" and "get off". What probably transpired in the length of a minute felt like the length of a grueling 45 minute class period. I could barely get up as my legs were shaking uncontrollably, my heart was racing like a metronome going at 130 BPM. I don't remember what happened next, but I sure remember the lesson I learned: It is important to be able to defend yourself physically, and we must defend and protect anyone who cannot fend for themselves for they are amongst the most vulnerable in our society. Looking back at that memory, I wonder how my peers felt and how/if that moment shaped their moral compass. I also remember bits and pieces from the 2008 election where then Sen. Barack Obama became the 44th President of the United States, making him the first African American to do so. We had a mock election in class and although I knew little about the candidates and where they stood on the issues, I made sure my peers cast their ballots for Obama over McCain because he looked like a nice guy. When the staff in the office announced the results of our mock election, the class and I lit up in jubilation. When Obama was later elected in the general election, I couldn't watch it live because the results came in way past my bedtime. My mother didn't wait to tell me the results the moment my little eyes opened and tried to shut again in a useless effort to get more sleep early in the morning. The most profound memory I took away from kindergarten wasn't a location or moment, it was instead the character of an individual who was my teacher; his name was Mr. Joe. He was a tall, soft-spoken Irishman who looked for the goodness in everyone. I remember Mr. Joe vividly because he not only listened to my many, many, many inquiries, but he also showed up at my house — a lot! Mr. Joe was the quintessential example of what happens when you put a community organizer in a classroom. He has since passed away, but his legacy lives on through each of his students. Including me.

1st Grade

THE MEMORIES I CARRY from first grade are faint. My teacher's name was Ms. Davis, an African American woman who ended up being one of a couple African American teachers I ever had. I remember being a class favorite when it came to choosing actors for mini-plays. "I don't know where you'll go in life, but I know that you've got a bright future in public speaking." Ms. Davis would say to me in front of the class as the children clapped in affirmation. I also remember discovering my distaste for schoolwork, especially on topics I wasn't interested in. The one prolific memory I still carry with me to this day was when Ms. Davis sat me down on a stool and talked to me about an issue I don't recall. The calm demeanor in her voice and the feeling of restorative practice at play put me at ease. It was my first memorable "meeting" with someone besides my parents and I loved every bit. I still feel warm inside, sharing it to this day.

2nd Grade

SECOND GRADE WAS THE first of many tough years for me. The love and patience I was used to receiving from previous educators like Mr. Joe and Ms. Davis seemed to fade quickly with my new teacher, Ms. Emilse. She was a strong Filipino mother who had previously had my older cousin as a student. I wish I could remember the catalyst of our relationship going awry, but despite my impressive recollection of past events, there are limitations. She once sat the class down to display each student's beautiful art projects. As she got to mine, the feeling of uncertainty and self-consciousness kicked in as my mind assumed my art piece was of inferior quality compared to my peers. She flipped to mine, took a hard look at it, and asked whose it was in a disingenuous way. As I nervously raised my shaky hand, she asked me to compare my work with my peers in front of them. "Look at yours and look at theirs." she said. "This is the best you have to offer?" She then admonished the class to be discreet in future interactions with me during art time. She proceeded to teach the class a recitation for when dealing with me to save themselves from the dark power I possessed called 'distraction'. Once students put their hand out mimicking a stop sign, she told them to say: "Go away Tiger!" they practiced it three times out loud with me sitting there. Ms. Emilse would also make smug comments to staff members like "If he were my child he would never see a TV". There was the time I burst into tears because she denied my genuine requests to get a drink of water. Despite the many things Ms. Emilse put me through, the scariest thing she'd do was call my parents due to the slightest provocation. The scary part wasn't going home to my disappointed parents. It was knowing that my teacher didn't know what to do with me and, in essence, gave up on trying to maintain a connection going forward. The bad kid narrative was settling in and I was slowly giving up on the prospect of ever succeeding in school. Once a teacher gives up on a student, that student will not succeed in said teacher's classroom. I get anxious looking back on memories like these because I'm reminded of how vulnerable young kids are and how reckless decisions made by adults can lead to the detriment of that young person not just in the current moment but going down the line.

Longfellow Shut Down (Budget Cuts)

BECAUSE OF LONGFELLOW SHUTTING down after my second-grade year, I transferred to the neighborhood school that rejected my sister and me a couple of years earlier. Seward Montessori was the better school, just not to me at the time. Seward had more funding and community engagement. The only problem; a diverse student body to a homogenous staff ratio.

3rd Grade

FOR SOME STUDENTS, TRANSFERRING to a different school can be tough. There are new sites to see, new smells, new social dynamics, etc. Whenever the Seward school anthem would play during an auditorium session, I would mumble the Longfellow school anthem because I was determined to never assimilate into the new school culture. My first experience with the complexity of gender was when a peer of mine, whom I thought was a boy, walked into the girl's bathroom. I quickly told them that was the girl's bathroom, and they replied with "I know". I later found out that my peer was a tomboy. The Montessori way of teaching is differs from your typical classroom structure. One noticeable difference is how the students address their teacher; not by Ms., or Mr., but directly by their first name. My new teacher's name was Millybeth. I vividly remember sitting in a circle during class toward the end of the day and getting a little sealed note from her. She handed it to me with a smile on her face and asked me to bring it back the next day with a parent's signature. I thought little of it, assuming it was just a preliminary piece of paperwork, until my older brother opened it and read it to me. The paper said that I "talked too much" and needed to focus more — I was shocked. Millybeth and Ms. Emilse had one thing in common; they didn't know what to do with me. Millybeth once kept me in from recess for an entire month in an attempt to get me to do work that I frankly didn't know how to do. During my parent-teacher conferences, Millybeth suggested to my mother that I see a psychologist due to me not performing at a level she deemed fit. My neighbor Janet, whom I call Auntie Janet, made it her job to make sure we completed our schoolwork, and that there was a clear line of communication between her and our teacher. She was compelled to help us in terms of having a powerful advocate/resource in academia. Janet was in the meeting with my mother and backed my teacher in trying to get me to see a psychologist. As I reminisced about this event with her on her porch around the time of the creation of this book, she apologized to me and explained her thought process at the time. The most traumatic thing that happened to me in Millybeth's classroom was when I was sent to time-out and mistakenly by another teacher in the room thought to have stuck up my middle finger. My teacher gasped and exclaimed "That's it! You're suspended, don't come back to school tomorrow" and went back to having a conversation with a student. Teachers don't have the power to suspend. Only the principal does. Because the principal wasn't notified and because I was mortified of telling my parents what the teacher said I showed up at school, the next day only to get a stern talking-to by the behavior specialist (a person who becomes increasingly relevant as the timeline continues). Millybeth gave up on me and it was clear in her increasingly short temper. A parent years later shared a conversation she had with

Millybeth about me. She told Millybeth, "That kid is going to be the president one day, you just wait and see." and Millybeth replied with "I don't know if he'll ever be able to settle down". Hearing that filled me with both jubilation and rage, but despite my mixed emotions, I was able to make one rational decision: Millybeth will not be invited to the White House under a Worku Administration.

4th & 5th Grade

I HAD THE SAME teacher for both the 4th and 5th grades. It was during these grades I developed an interest in government. A state legislator invited our class to the state capitol and the amount of detail in the capitol's architecture wasn't lost on me. I ran for student government in both grades, but failed to garnish enough support from my classmates to get elected. My teacher, Lynda, understood me. I spoke with Lynda after nearly ten years during the creation of this passage. We laughed, shed a few tears, and caught up on all the lost time.

Middle School (6th, 7th, & 8th Grades)

MOST OF MY LEARNING in middle school didn't take place in the classroom. I enjoyed studying the social and institutional dynamics of my school more than I studied the Pythagorean theorem. I discovered that my lack of work ethic in the classroom wasn't because I was innately slow or lazy, but because I simply didn't care for what was being taught — mainly because the vast majority of it was useless. The comical part is no matter how much work I failed to do, I never fell short of successfully challenging a teacher on any given subject. A couple of my classmates would congregate before every class session, then make their way to my desk to ask if I could argue with the teacher. To this day, I wonder if my peers found it amusing or if they just needed some cover to use their phones. During my eighth-grade year, I got into an altercation with a student, which ended with me filing a civil rights case against my school. The details about what led up to the civil rights case and what happened after are so extensive, I've dedicated an entire chapter to it later on in the book. The 2016 presidential primaries took place during my eighth-grade year and, as you can imagine, folks were passionate — very passionate about their preferred candidates. An Independent Senator from the state of Vermont not only caught my attention with his "radical" views but fundamentally changed the trajectory of my life. If there was a single person or message that got me into politics, it revolved around Bernie Sanders. Although he ended up losing the primary, he won the long-term ideological battle to bring about a social, economic, and political revolution in the United States of America.

9th Grade

NINTH GRADE WAS ONE of my more comical years. I was one of the kids that watched High School Musical 1, 2, and 3 before the school year began assuming my experience would be somewhat similar, only to find out it was all just a mirage. I went to South High School, and the mascot was and still is a Tiger — I was reminded of it every day either through new interactions, or corny jokes by friends. My brother attended and graduated from South several years before me, so the school itself wasn't completely foreign. My

guard was up going into high school due to the abuse
I underwent at Seward. Any anguish I felt of an elab-
orate scheme to make my life a living hell by staff was
quickly put to rest after I made personal connections
with my teachers. For me, the challenge became fit-
ting in amongst my peers in a way that allowed me
to be me. The level of maturity I exhibited entering
high school was light years ahead of my peers; it was
evident in the interactions I had with staff. A month
into my freshman year, a brunette by the name of
Josephine caught my attention. She was also a freshman. I mustered up the courage to reach out to her
on social media, hoping she would give an unpol-
ished young man like myself a chance. She responded
with callus, instantly shutting me down. The feeling
of shock and fear that pulsed through my body when
she continued to berate me for having the audacity
to even think about being in a relationship with her
was something that took a couple of years to shake
off. When she recorded my texts and posted it to her
Instagram account, bragging about how "mean" she
was, I finally understood the idiom: 'don't judge a
book by its cover'. It's one thing to reject someone,
but it's another thing to completely humiliate them. I

do, however, appreciate the thick skin that I was able
to develop from that event. Even though half of the
freshman class of girls liked her inconsiderate posts
humiliating me on social media, I was able to finish
out the rest of my 9th-grade year in good social standing with the majority of my peers and teachers.

10th Grade

PROCRASTINATION WASN'T JUST SOMETHING I practiced, it was something I mastered at this point.
Whenever my teachers asked me why I wasn't keeping up with any of the homework, I responded with
the excuse that it was a "sophomore slump" and that
it was perfectly normal. The reason my parents and
teachers weren't too worried about my academic slip
was because there was a clear understanding of where
that time and energy were going. All my life, I was
told that being an excellent student academically and
minding my own business was the key to success.
Until my tenth-grade year, I was under the illusion
that our school system ran entirely on a meritocracy
basis. I pretty much completely gave up on schoolwork and focused on what I truly loved: politics. My

Cs became trophies. I sought comfort in knowing that school wasn't hard for me; I just never cared enough to try. A major event that started during my sophomore year was the detention of children from their parents at the southern border and the racist threat against DACA recipients. I asked my Latin friend to translate a PowerPoint I created in Spanish and I hosted an event in my school's auditorium called "How To Protect Dreamers" explaining to students what their rights were if they were ever approached by ICE and how to help someone who they'd suspect to be in danger of getting deported. I still have a pocket constitution booklet to this day from the pile that we handed out to students. School shootings were also a common occurrence at this time, so I led a march to city hall, where Rep. Ilhan Omar's daughter and I led a couple of chants. During my tenth-grade year, I turned my infatuation with the political world into a passion for fighting for others.

11th Grade

AFTER A MEDIOCRE ACADEMIC performance during my tenth-grade year, I felt the need to improve my academic standing to look more desirable for colleges. The ACT was just around the corner, and I found myself in a bit of a predicament. Some may wonder why I couldn't just balance both academics and politics; it wasn't that simple. There was a continued assault on our society's most vulnerable. I couldn't be in good conscious spend hours of my day working on keep-busy work. Despite my intention to do better academically, a new movement was hatched. The movement brought everyone to the battlefield with equal interest because it didn't start in defense of any one person, place, or thing. The movement that developed, spearheaded by youth, was in defense of our planet. Greta Thunberg, a young climate activist from Sweden, decided to go on strike from a school outside her country's capital to prove a point about the complacency and complicity of world leaders on the issue of climate change. Like many of the world's youth, I heard the call and lobbied our elected officials to do something. Since Washington D.C. was out of reach for me, I had to rally legislators at my state's capital in Saint Paul. With a small group of kids from all across the state of Minnesota, I co-sponsored a piece of legislation called the MN Green New Deal. During my junior year, I deepened my love for government and turned a part-time gig into a full-time job.

12th Grade

AFTER ACCEPTING THE FACT that my poor academic standing was all but written in stone. I decided to focus on leaving behind an empowering social legacy at my school — not by getting blackout drunk at parties, or smoking marijuana until I questioned my very existence on this earth. I decided to start a Black Student Union because I saw the need that black and brown students had, not only at my school, but across the nation. A need for unbiased instruction, a need for stronger comradery amongst each other and a need for belonging in the building. The unique relationships that I built with certain staff members and teachers over the years were finally starting to pay off. I had the privilege of leaving the building whenever I wanted, not going to class whenever I wanted. I even got a daily briefing on what some of the latest teacher/staff drama was about. A week before the start of our Thanksgiving Break several quarrels broke out in bathrooms and hallways all across the knew it, it was circulating throughout all the school's social cliques. People were interested in making it happen; either because it meant students finally had the collective power to stick it to the administration, or because some saw this as an opportunity to get out of class and cause some 'good trouble' — maybe both. On the day of the protest, the principal met with me privately and struck up a pacifying tone. He worried that the protest may spiral out of control, but I assured him that students were going to behave. Once the protest started, children packed the halls refusing to go to class and staff were nervously standing by in the event things took a turn for the worst. Once the students packed the halls for a bit, I gave a quick speech as to how powerful the demonstration was and dismissed everyone to continue their regularly scheduled day. The next day as I walked into the building, one of our school's security guards pulled me aside and told me that the principal met with a group of staff and security and asked, "How could one kid have that much power". The pass ban was no more. After invigorating the student body once, I pulled together a team of passionate students and we were able to do it again. We called for one more protest in response to the continued racism shown by some staff. It was after the two protests and the successful launch of the school's first Black Student Union that I was able to rest assured that my legacy would be left behind through the organizing of students for classes to come. I was going to graduate with a 2.2 GPA and a smile on my face because I knew that I was ready to take on the world. One major catastrophic event occurred that put the rest of my senior year on halt and threw the world for a ride. My class, the class of 2020, would be remembered not for our accolades but for our sacrifice. This event and the other major event following it had such an influential impact on not only my educational experience but the world at large.

COVID-19

ABOUT HALFWAY THROUGH MY senior year, the COVID-19 pandemic hit. I remember hearing about it through CNN on Monday and being out of school for the rest of the year by Friday. The pandemic upended society as we knew it. Everything in America shutdown, and face masks became the new norm. Prom and other senior events were canceled. What was once thought of as minute became a reality when our graduation ceremony was done virtually. Some seniors felt hurt about the pandemic but I, on the other hand, felt blessed for a number of reasons:

- I had absolutely no loyalty to any of the cultural coming of age activities that we missed — I was ready to get my diploma and be on my way.

- The pandemic was killing thousands of people a day, and I felt privileged to have the resources and the precautions in place to keep me and my loved one's safe.

- The pandemic blew away any shelter the adults in our life could provide us with and showed us what the world had to offer. I was mesmerized by how my generation would be remembered and how we would be molded by this event as the leaders of tomorrow.

The Murder of George Floyd

WHILE EVERYONE WAS TRAPPED at home because of the COVID-19 pandemic, it felt like life was on pause. I remember shopping at Target in the produce aisle when I got a text from my neighbors asking me if I wanted to go to a protest on 38th and Chicago.

I responded by asking what the protest was about and before I could put my phone back in my pocket; I received a call from my sister. She explained that the police killed an unarmed black man and that it was all caught on tape. I thanked her for the update, got a text from my neighbor corroborating the incident, and quickly finished my shopping, eager to see the video at home. When I got home and played the video on YouTube in front of my sister and uncle, I couldn't believe what I was watching. In my city, near my neighborhood; the police department, whom I already knew was racist, committed a public execution with such callous. Bystanders were pleading with and admonishing the officers to show mercy on George Floyd. Hearing the words "I can't breathe" and "Momma" repeatedly sheared through every American's complacency and neglect of racial issues. I instantly responded "yes" to my neighbor's text. We met downstairs with a few other neighbors and we descended on the site of George Floyd's killing, accompanied by thousands of other Minnesotans. The protest quickly moved to Lake Street where the Third Precinct was located, and after days of unrest and demonstrations, unfortunately, a good portion of school. The principle in a desperate attempt to try and regain some order in the building sent out an email to teachers telling them to deny students a pass to go to the bathroom, or to go to the water fountain for a drink — it was and still is ludicrous to me that young adults needed permission to take care of their basic human rights. The problem with the new rule was that many teachers had a bias towards children of color, and that rule just exacerbated the amount of times children of color were denied a pass across the board. White students took notice of this and spoke out at certain times about it, one of my teachers recounted a moment where they asked a white student how they felt about the 'no pass rule' and the student replied by saying "It doesn't matter to me, I'm white. The teachers don't care if I leave the room". After hearing that statement and reading the email profusely, I organized a protest to lift the ban on passes. Skin color aside, I felt it was asinine that seventeen- and eighteen-year-olds needed to ask permission to take a number two. I remember going home and feeling a weird type of energy. The energy was powerful and made me feel happy but also anxious at the same time. I created a poster that I later posted to social media, and before I

South Minneapolis was burned to the ground. During the peaceful protests, the police responded with a disproportionate amount of force. I was tear-gassed twice and hit in the lower abdominal with a rubber bullet. This event was a turning point in American history because racial inequality was finally something that all people were starting to see. Public opinion polls that were conducted at this time showed that there seemed to be an epiphany going on in the minds of many White Americans. I wanted there to be peace in America, but I wanted everyone to be at peace — as I still do.

Chapter 2:

Retribution

To feel its warmth...

WHAT HAPPENED DURING MY eighth-grade year reshaped my entire perception of schooling. I was forced to re-analyze old memories and cautiously proceed in making new ones. Years later, I came across a quote that couldn't have been more accurate in describing the events that took place during my eighth-grade year: "The village must embrace the child or the child will burn down the village to feel its warmth". I titled this chapter "Retribution" because the innate response to being treated the way I was would be to immediately seek it. At first, I did. As I detail this chapter with enraging instances and insurgent moments, I ask that you apply a systemic lens to understand why certain things played out the way they did. Although I had been subjected to things that no student should be subjected to, I felt that the best way to settle the score would be to attack the problem at its core; and so I did. If you feel up in arms about what you're about to read, I urge you to do the same.

November 20th, 2015:

THE SCHOOL DAY STARTED like any other regular school day for me. I showed up half-awake; I shuffled through the halls to get to my first hour, and I expected another boring day of school. I had previously heard reports of a boy named Leonitus wanting to fight me. I shrugged off the rumors mainly because I hadn't been in contact with him, nor did I have any issues with him. Leonitus and I were in the same first hour during my sixth-grade year. One day in sixth grade, he showed up at school with cuts on his arm and a knife tucked away in his pocket. He came up to me and another student telling us about his plans to end his life; an idea that was very foreign to me at the time. The student and I tried to convince him to tell the teacher to seek help, but our wisdom proved ineffective in convincing his adamantine clandestine spirit. After carefully weighing the dilemma of being labeled a 'snitch' or being complicit in someone's demise, I chose to privately alert the teacher. Leonitus was then taken away from class by Norman — remember that name — and suspended for bringing a weapon to school. Another clear sign of how botched our education system is. We didn't speak until seventh grade. In seventh grade, I asked out a girl named Tay only to be told no. I then tried my luck again with her twin sister Emmalise and got an enthusiastic yes. The next day I saw Emmalise talking to a sad Leonitus by the tree and later asked her what was wrong. She told me she'd rejected him and that he felt upset about our new romantic escapade. I didn't speak to him about it, mainly because Emma and my relationship lasted a whopping three days. I had one more encounter with him that year when he came up to me and asked me out. I respectfully declined because I have always been straight. My next interaction with him was during my eighth-grade year on November 20th, 2015. Leading up to this incident, I was involved in several school activities like an exclusive leadership group and the nationally awarded chess team that I was the best player of. I didn't have the highest academic marks, but I had never been seriously disciplined until this incident. I remember a weird churning feeling in my stomach a couple of minutes before recess began that day. I finished my lunch and exited out the doors, unknowing of how much my eighth-grade year would take a turn for the worst. On the way inside after recess, I remember seeing a swarm of kids gather around me. Leonitus appeared from the group and maligned me. Instead of trying to intervene, students mocked and instigated us to satisfy their barbaric middle school minds. I remember looking into his eyes, seeing the fear, and witnessing the peer pressure at work. The question that kept going through my mind was: "Why?". What could I have done to compel this student to want to physically harm me? As the atmosphere grew more intense, I knew a skirmish was inevitable. Leonitus swung and missed. I quickly grappled him and took him to the ground. As he tried to get up, I pinned his shoulders to the ground and countered his strikes with strikes of my own. Then, his friend Langorian jumped on top and inadvertently started a dog pile after my friends quickly moved in, too. After what felt like an eternity, we were broken up and separated. I was immediately brought into a small interrogation-like room where I was left for about 30 minutes. A woman named Meg and Norman walked into the room. Without asking if I was ok, they handed me a piece of paper and told me to write down my version of events. While I was writing my side of the story, Norman reached for the phone on the desk and called my mother. I could tell she was worried and anxious based on his responses to her. One thing that stuck out to me during that call was when he looked up and down at me and said: "He looks fine to me from what I can tell." and handed me the phone. I reassured my mother that I was feeling fine and told her not to worry. I then put the phone back on its handset. After finishing my account of what happened, Meg read my paper and told me to re-write it. I explained that this was my account, and re-writing it would corrupt their analysis of what happened. She was adamant about me rewriting it, so I asked what exactly she wanted from a second copy.

She said that she wanted me to write an admission of
guilt. Perplexed, I raised my voice and said, "But you
weren't there. Why would you think I started it?!".
Norman then abruptly said "watch your tone." and
asked me to apologize. Unsatisfied with my forced
apology, Norman said, "We'll try that again later." and
explained that he believed, based on his "30 years" of
experience, that I was the one who instigated everything from the start. At that moment, I knew things
weren't being handled right. I gathered enough courage to say that I wouldn't re-write my story, and that
I already wrote what I needed to write. Both Norman
and Meg walked out of the room, leaving me to ponder over what was in store for this process. After about
ten minutes, Norman walked in and asked me to come
with him. We walked over to the principal's office
where my Mother and Meg were waiting for me. As
Norman and Meg persisted in expressing their false
narrative about what happened, my mother insisted
that I didn't instigate or want an altercation. Only the
principal of a school can suspend a student and since
the principal was absent that day, they sent me home
and asked me to come back to school the following
school day; which was a Monday with an admission

of guilt. I went home, explained the situation to my older brother, and stuck with what I had previously written — the truth.

November 23rd, 2015:

MY BROTHER ACCOMPANIED ME to what we expected would be a meeting between the principal and us. Once we got to school that morning, I felt more at ease thinking that I'd be able to rely upon my past non-violent record and my honest verbal explanation of what happened, unfortunately; it was not to be. As we made our way to the principal's office, Norman and Meg met us. They welcomed my brother and sat with us until the principal arrived. Tammatha (the principal) entered the room and said: "It sounds like you made an unfortunate decision. I think we should move on and try again on Wednesday." implying that there would be a two-day suspension. She then unexpectedly pulled up my transcript and said: "It looks like you've got some work to do in your classes." I instantly stated that my transcripts weren't germane to what was being discussed and got cut off with this scathing remark: "Ah, Tiger, everything we do here at

Seward is about academics." I remember leaving that meeting in defeat. The feeling of being too weak or inarticulate to fight injustice loomed over me. Some kids would picture what happened to me as a dream scenario. My parent wasn't mad at me, I had two days to play video games. What's there to sweat? For some reason, I couldn't let it go. I didn't just want to pursue other alternatives to seeking justice for entertainment reasons; I was compelled to stand up and fight for what I believed was right. A 74-year-old-democratic socialist who was seeking the Democratic nomination at the time inspired me. Once we got home, I asked my brother if there was anything I could do to overrule the school's decision. He sat me down and had 'the talk' with me; anticipating I'd have an easier time swallowing a pill that too many in this country have to swallow. At first, I figured I'd be better off just cutting losses short until I got multiple Snapchats from my friends at school asking where I was. I explained that Leonitus and I got suspended and wouldn't be back until Wednesday. Then, to my astonishment, I was told that Leonitus and Langorian were at school, bragging about how they took me out. The school was also going around disciplining students who jumped in to get Langorian off me. After I heard that Leonitus and Langorian were back in school, I began my investigation into how the school handled the altercation. Instead of going off pretenses, I had one of my friends go up and interview Leonitus about what happened to him after the fight. The report I got back was enraging. While they took me straight into an interrogation room, Leonitus was taken straight to the nurse's office as a safety precaution. While I sat in a room anxiously awaiting my fate, tender words reassured him. My mother had to come to school and pick me up. Leonitus got to take the bus home. They found me guilty. They found him innocent. Once I heard the report, I knew I was going to fight my suspension, although I didn't have any basic legal understanding or any obvious resources at my disposal. I went back to my brother and insisted on appealing the school's ruling. I was expecting him to write me off, but he looked into my eyes and said, "Ok, I'll call the district." I was taken aback by how quickly a plan opened up. I hadn't thought about the district before, but the thought of dissenting or rebelling filled my body with adrenaline. I thought that justice was right around the corner and that if it were this easy, we may very well be in a post-racial America. Little did I know, I was in for a fight. After my brother's conversation with the district, he came into my room and informed me of the district's decision to stay neutral. The school district said that it's seldom for a school's decision to be overturned or even reviewed by the district and that other legal options would be more prudent to appeal the case. I was crushed. My brother reassured me that the suspension wouldn't hurt my record and that it was normal to get in trouble as a juvenile. The most important thing for me was knowing I had my family's trust and support. As he left the room I thought to myself, "well at least you tried." Half of me wanted to concede defeat, but the other half simply couldn't. As I thought through what the woman from the district said, my neighbor David came to mind. I befriended David's nephew when I was much younger. David knew my family very well and he just so happened to be a lawyer. I thought to myself, what's the harm in asking him to hear my story? I knew and still know him to be an ardent fighter for justice. He led many anti-war and civil rights demonstrations in the sixties. He was a union steward back in college, and we engaged in several philosophical conversations that enlightened the both of us. For me, it was obvious that he was the guy for the job. Without telling my family, I went over to his house and explained the situation. He was eager to help and asked for time to review some options. I went home feeling accomplished, but braced myself for what I then expected to be an arduous process.

The rest of the case:

DAVID GOT BACK TO me the next day with an option of a formal civil rights complaint. The word civil rights rang a bell, but a "formal complaint" hadn't. Once explained, I agreed and informed my family of my decision. My family had a mixed reaction; there was some humor, some angst. I assured them that this was what I wanted and got their blessing to proceed. I went to David and started strategizing how we could most effectively prove our case. I mentioned that the school had forced folks to write admissions of guilt and so he suggested I get witness statements of my own. The task of collecting witness statements during the school day in plain cite was no easy feat to accomplish, but I was determined to seek justice and so I collected eleven witness statements hand-written and signed. The district's attorney agreed to a meeting with me, David, and the school staff, but backtracked to protect any wrongdoing. Once I told some of my peers about the process, my popularity shot up. I was known as the kid who sued the school. I thought the process would play itself out and that the school would have some remorse for what they did. I never in a million years thought I would be subjected to the type of retaliatory attacks that were waged. It started with smear comments like when I would raise my hand in class to ask a clarifying question and get responses like "Sue me." or "Are you going to take me to court?" I once reported an incident of a kid harassing another kid and got an in-school suspension — even though I reported the incident that had nothing to do with me. The vice-principal later told the boy that he should steer clear of me because I'm a very "manipulative" person. I remember Meg asking me to step into the principal's office because she felt "intimidated" by how I was looking at her. I was also given a one-day suspension by the principal because I was playing with snow. My mother and David were in the meeting with me when she asked me to not return to school the next day — it was later denied and never recorded on my official record, which is illegal. Perhaps the most memorable experience for me during this entire process was when my counselor asked my mother to come in to talk about high school options, but ambushed us with a negative meeting with all my teachers present; which Meg presided over. I was such a "good kid" before this civil rights case started, but because I chose to challenge a decision through legal channels, I was this delinquent who needed to be disciplined. During the meeting, my mother asked a question that left the room silent: "If he's such a burden, then why haven't I been contacted about it?" That question single-handedly exposed the entire purpose of the meeting. I never got any complaints from my teachers before that meeting and I've never gotten any complaints since. I left Seward with the case still pending. The most scathing thing for me was the magnitude of how many other children faced similar responses. I decided to stand up and fight with some sense of accomplishment and dignity, but so many were forced to succumb to defeat. Just like this instance has altered me, their experiences have altered them too, either consciously or subconsciously. I found out the results of

the complaint about halfway through my freshman
year. David called me and informed me of our loss.
Proving a civil rights violation isn't easy, especially if
the defendant will pay millions to maintain inno-
cence. As an eighth-grader, I had the near-impossible
task of collecting signatures, being vigilant of adults
watching my every move, all while trying to get an
education. A lot of these bouts turned into a 'he said,
they said' situation. Because I couldn't prove definitely
that I was discriminated against. The OCR ruled to
dismiss the case. David asked if I wanted to appeal,
but I couldn't put myself through that process again.
I decided that since I was no longer attending Seward,
it would be more prudent to move on and put it in my
past. So I said no. Earlier, I explained why I felt the
word "retribution" was an appropriate title for this
chapter. Retribution is often frowned upon by many
cultures. We're taught to 'turn the other cheek' because
'an eye for an eye makes the entire world blind' and
indeed sometimes that school of thought reigns superior. Had I sought retribution by cursing out teachers
or assaulting students, then you'd be reading a different story. Some may argue that I didn't seek retribution, rather I sought accountability. The two mustn't

be confused; rather than viewing it through an either-or lens, I choose to view it through a both-and lens. Retribution is a form of justice. I believe it becomes dangerous when folks hide their intentions, sacrificing good counsel, and transparency. It would be naive to turn the other cheek away from an unjust system that makes you complicit in the suffering of others. In my case, the retribution hasn't stopped. Seward may have won the battle, but there is no way they'll win the war. Some may attribute this mindset to an unhealthy overabundance of trauma. Although I sustained trauma during this process, I cannot go back and undo it. The school may have caused me trauma, but I caused it trauma by taking it on and putting every teacher and administrator on notice. My experience and the experience of other students aren't mutually exclusive. I think everyone carries some trauma from their childhood. Many of the trauma that takes place in schools goes forgotten because our society has forced us to normalize it. Our schools do not operate in the way technology or motors do; updates are much slower and upgrades happen once in every three lifetimes. If we continue to ignore American schooling's rugged edges, then we create the same environment for our children not because it's a 'coming of age' moment but because we lack the empathy to stop their suffering — shame on us. Teachers have the near-impossible task of facilitating a classroom for eight hours a day while understanding the needs and dynamics of every student in their classroom(s). We ask them to do an extraordinary job on such an ordinary salary — many would beg to differ that it's even "ordinary". One hundred percent of teachers would speak up if it means helping their students succeed. However, not even one percent will sacrifice their job and starve their family, or lose their home to prove a point — who would? Even though much of my experience has been rough, I've decided to see past the nuance and focus on the problem at its core. Our teachers need more pay, they need enough job security to be able to speak up and speak their mind, they need more training, they need to reflect the changing demographics of their students, and they need an upgraded school system. Students also have a near-impossible task. They are expected to spend twelve years of their life memorizing things that will either be forgotten or nugatory later on in life. Our kids call out this bluff every single day. They go to school and are often bombarded with comments like "You're just lazy" or "You actually will need a lot of this stuff." which are lies. In today's society, children are much savvier than adults in terms of handling technology. The world is relying more and more on tech, yet we continue to insist that large textbooks and paper packets of homework are the superior options for learning. Technology has the power to create a new subject, yet we continue to treat it as a secondary source for pleasure. Our students need more play, they need a platform and a seat at the table to voice their opinion, they need a better curriculum, they need staff members who reflect on their experiences, and they need an upgraded school system. The school system also has a near-impossible task. It's expected to produce results without proper care or maintenance. It's been around for about five centuries. If you look at an old picture of an American school classroom, then you'll see a striking resemblance to classrooms today. We've often looked to developing countries to justify our setup. Indeed, some form of school is better than no school at all. For some reason, we cannot look to countries that get better results than us, like Finland and Norway. We're caught in a system of justifying instead of rectifying. Our schooling system needs more pressure to change, it needs to stop testing students for competition, it needs to stop being a political talking point for both sides of the aisle, it needs to prioritize a public model, and it needs to be upgraded. How can my case have a big enough impact to change things? It can't. It didn't. We often think about landmark cases as the end all be all of any given situation. Brown v. Board of Education was integral to winning the legal battle for integration, but it alone didn't change hearts and minds. The foot soldiers were individuals deciding to send their kids to white schools. My case didn't achieve landmark status because it wasn't intended to. I believe that a minor act of defiance can change the world. I stood up not for vanity but justice. This battle was a part of a much larger conflict taking place. What was first fueled by retribution turned into a much larger yearning for truth and fairness. Since middle school, I've run into some of the staff who tormented me. I've run into Norman multiple times. The most recent run-in with him was after twelfth grade. I was out riding on my vespa when I saw him smoking a cigarette on the corner next to the school. He flagged me down and so I pulled over to chat. After chatting about current events, I told him that I had forgiven him for what he did and wish to move past it. He said that he'd already moved past it. He also mentioned that he believed a large part of it was a "normal developmental milestone." I internally disagreed with that notion, but before I could put forth my analysis, he was called to do a task, so our conversation abruptly ended. I never ran into Meg again, but my first employer was a relative of hers. I explained to her some of my experiences and she shared with me a conversation the two of them had about her children on a walk. Meg asked if she knew where she wanted to send her kids — whom were infants at the time. She replied she didn't know yet and Meg responded by saying, "You have to send your kids to Seward. We need more white kids."

As the Vice-President of the Seward Neighborhood Group during my twelfth-grade year, I was in a virtual call with Tammatha, who implored us to reject the district's new plan to gut Seward's middle school program because of equity concerns. I mentioned the disproportionate disciplinary rates amongst students based on skin color and got the snappy remark that this was a "normal developmental milestone". That remark watered down the bias in play and erased the premise of my civil rights case. The irony of the entire situation was that the woman who worked so hard to gaslight me was now imploring me to help save a piece of the school. The same school that isolated me from the rest of the students to abuse power. I chose not to ardently fight the district. The middle school was cut.

I didn't choose to support the destruction of Seward's middle school, purely out of retribution. I listened and analyzed what both sides had to say and felt that although some may disagree with the district's plan — at least they had a plan. In a district where racial inequities are staunch, I believed that a plan as radical as the districts' was not only worthwhile, but needed. At the beginning of the chapter, I talked about how I sought justice in a way that attacked the problem at its core. In many ways I did, and in many ways I still am. By involving myself in deciding on such an altering policy decision, I brought a perspective that rarely gets heard. By staying out of trouble and not falling victim to the negative statistics, I'm attacking the school to prison pipeline problem. In writing this book and sharing these details, I'm attacking the lack of transparency problem that's prevalent in too many of our schools. We mustn't focus solely on Seward Montessori. I urge folks to consider how their local schools or former schools may be conducting business in similar ways. If you're a parent, consider how this may affect your child or other children. Get involved! If you're a current student, then understand your power as an individual and the collective power of the entire student body. If you're a former student, then consider attending some school board meetings and volunteering your time at local schools. If you're a teacher, then please attempt to hold your problematic colleagues/administrations accountable. Despite my litigious and storied past with public schools, I still have hope for them. I do not believe that there is a more fair or comprehensive method of learning for all of our students in the market. By radically changing how we engage with the system, not only will we save our public schools, but we will have a more grateful and educated generation to fall back on. The temptation for retribution must transmute into a concentration for the greater good.

Chapter 3:

My Friend Nazir

You've got a friend in me.

EDICATING A CHAPTER IN your book to someone is a testament to how strong your bond is with them. At this point, Nazir and I have only known each other for a relatively short period of time. We come from different generations, different cultures, different states, yet there is a strong bond that unites us. The only thing stronger is the force that brought us together. Despite many of Nazir's positive characteristics, it isn't his wit or compassion that has compelled me to write this chapter; instead, it's what he represents. When I first met Nazir, I'd already had my foot planted pretty deep in politics. I joined an organization alongside other youth throughout my state, advocating for an expeditious solution to climate change. I had operated in a way that many politicians, unfortunately, operate in today. I overvalued the camera and devalued the work. Some of the adults who orbited the organization treated the youth as pets in a petting zoo rather than young leaders at different stages of their advocacy. I, alongside a couple other youth, stood out from the pack and so were given more opportunities, e.g., press conferences or backroom meetings with influential people. I went from a young, well-intentioned activist to a cynical dynamo. One of the youth suggested I meet with a man named Nazir who was doing work for a local DSA chapter. I agreed, eager to hear more about the notorious term called socialism. After briefly chatting on the phone with Nazir to set up a time to meet, I assumed this would be the typical interaction I had with adults; which ended with me being used. I was wrong. Nazir was different. Instead of having a direct ask, he was able to read through my tainted aspirations and was compelled to take on an advisory role.

There was a specific need that I had that I couldn't pinpoint at that moment. I needed an advisor and a friend. Nazir was there at the right time and he is filling that need to this day. He had several qualifications to take on the role. Nazir grew up in New York City; the son of immigrants from India. After graduating from high school at sixteen, he attended Harvard University alongside Pete Buttigieg. He traveled the country in '08 for Obama and eventually moved to Minneapolis where union organizing, amongst other things, became his signature craft. I recognized early on that there was a lot to learn. Our conversations about life rekindled my love for authentic communication. Seeking advice never felt like a burden. It was more comical and satisfying. One of the most profound changes that took place in my life during this period was the expansion of my social circle. There was an entire world of folks with similar stories doing similar work across Minneapolis & Saint Paul. I never really socially fit in at school, so by the time my senior year rolled around 99% of my social interactions were taking place outside of school. Nazir introduced me to his immediate group of friends and before I knew it, I found myself regularly talking to Isuru, Bol, Jacob,

Kong, Wako, etc. I remember the feeling of compan-
ionship during the many feasts we would have at
Isuru's house, or the humor in sharing stories during
car rides with Bol, Jacob, and Wako, or the insightful-
ness during strategizing sessions with Kong. It would
be an understatement to describe my relationship
with these individuals as plain friendships. Instead,
we bonded as brothers. I would count on them in
times of need and they would do the same vice versa.
There's an old saying that goes "Show me who your
friends are, and I will show you who you are." naturally
that applies to political views as well. pre-Nazir, I considered myself to be a moderate democrat. I held that
view not based on the content of what I believed, but
because of the uncertainty of what I believed. I had
advanced political views but lacked the audience to
discuss them with. A lot of what I felt was based on
my gut feeling. My strong feelings were usually
watered down by the then-popular notion that a good
belief is a compromised belief. I admired people based
on how they were perceived rather than what they
stood for. All of that changed with my new social circles. Not only did I have an audience to chat with, but
I also had a plethora of different ideas presented to

me. I gained confidence in my political stances, earning my political stripes. It was ok to think that everyone should have quality healthcare and I could have a discussion with Isuru on it. It was ok to think workers shouldn't face any rode block in wanting to create a union and I could chat with Bol or Kong about it. It was ok to hold police departments accountable for some of their reprehensible actions and I could chat with Jacob or Wako about it. It was ok to become active and organzine around these beliefs with Nazir and others. This marked an inflection point for me. Instead of going down the typical route politicians go down, I was able to truly understand why I was in the fight in the first place — many politicians have lost sight. It was also a humbling experience. Competition was no longer the name of the game; solidarity was. When I showed up in spaces, it wasn't to talk or take up space, but to help in whatever way I could. If I wasn't needed for help, then I simply showed up as a spectator. From all of this, my organizing philosophy was reborn. It became abundantly obvious that I didn't need to prove anything because I was already accepted for who I was. Pre-Nazir I always had to prove my worth (still the case sometimes.) because one who is deemed unworthy gets looked over and forgotten about. During my first interactions in organizing with Nazir, I could show up in these circles and be heard and appreciated while reciprocating the same feelings towards others. No mischievous calculation was needed. I also learned about the importance of hard work. So much of politics revolves around press conferences, posturing, social media posts, but little light is shined on the work that must be done behind the scenes. The emails that have to be written then re-written, the compromises that need to be made, the introductions and follow-ups that need to take place. Politicians who make it higher up the ladder don't necessarily need to engage in a significant chunk of this behavior because they have staff who take care of it. Nazir clarified that if I were to engage in politics, then I'd engage in its most authentic form. Perhaps many politicians lose their authenticity because they aren't constantly reminded of why they're in politics through their work. It was during a Friendsgiving dinner at Isuru's that put everything into perspective. Kong brought sticky rice with sausage and serenaded us with traditional Hmong songs. Isuru made Fish Ambul Thiyal and talked about his childhood stories

from Sri Lanka. Jacob and Bol brought drinks. Nazir
started and facilitated the many unforgettable board
games we played that night. Through brotherhood
and story, I was able to rekindle a dormant spark in
me that has only grown more powerful since. That
temporary high all extraverts get from social interaction turned into a long-lasting drive that few get to
experience. The very basis of being conservative or
liberal depends on who your friends are. Personalities
are one thing, but identity is another. I was sitting in
a room with a diverse group of people with diverse
opinions and stories. Folks who are more conserva-
tive-minded loathe significant amounts of change.
Folks who are more liberal-minded accept change and
are often the driving force behind it. In terms of social
connection, I think it is more difficult for many con-
servatives to build diverse friend groups because of
their innate closed-off environments. When you are
exposed to a significant amount of diversity, you are
forced to change and adapt to connect and understand
those around you. For example, if you travel to another
country, you will adhere to the traditions and norms
while you're there; so the same has to apply to connect
with others from different backgrounds. One mustn't

compromise their true identity too much because then one wouldn't be authentic to oneself or others. It ultimately depends on the level of respect one is willing to show in the name of harmony. My friend groups have always resembled a mini-United Nations and I believe it's because of the principles instilled in me at a young age: Treat everyone with respect, nobody's too young to teach, and nobody's too old to learn. Everyone is unique in their own right.

Something else that stood out from my group of friends was age. I was the outlier because I was significantly younger. I've never been able to make friends with kids my age. In school, I would spark up more conversations with the teachers and staff members than I would with my peers. If I saw a new staff member during lunch duty or recess duty, I would go up and introduce myself, knowing that this interaction was the first of many. I was more gravitated towards adults because I quickly came to realize that with friendship came preferential treatment, but also more mental stimuli. I wasn't interested in talking about last night's cartoon or which Pokemon card was the strongest. I wanted to dive deep into many of the world's challenging problems. Adults gave me the greatest opportunity to exercise my knowledge and wit and in some cases the opportunity to mentally spar; I was a precocious kid. Hanging with older folks wasn't such an aberration for me. Bol and Jacob were the closest to my age, and they were at least five years older than me. Nazir, Isuru, and Kong have at least a decade over me. Although I've become accustomed to hanging with older folks, I haven't forgotten the life experiences that I have yet to experience, that they already have. That's why I make sure to listen to and heed their advice. There are also times where I advise, and luckily my friends listen. Young people are often discounted because of their age, but the principle that was instilled in me at a young age "Nobody's too young to teach, and nobody's too old to learn." holds a significant amount of weight in my head. Ageism is often a term referred to as the mistreatment of older folks, but it still applies to younger folks as well. As stated earlier, Nazir attended Harvard at sixteen. Some parents cannot imagine sending their sixteen-year-olds to the grocery store, let alone letting them enroll at the most prestigious universities in the world. Harvard didn't stop Nazir from attending because of his age. They

welcomed him because of his merit. Many would find
it asinine for an institution to block a person because
of their age, yet many non-academic institutions do
it to this day. The rule that you can drink at twenty-one
but have to wait until the age of twenty-five to run for
a seat in the House of Representatives, and until the
age of thirty to run for the Senate, is antiquated and
poorly constructed. The fact that sometimes for an
entry-level job, you need a significant amount of experience that isn't provided to you during your schooling
is detached and unsustainable. Many of these things
are regarded by the public as a hassle, yet they continue to be enforced in full force due to the lack of
public call out. Networking is another crucial reason
I was more inclined to make friends with older folks.
I understood at a young age that in today's world, it
isn't what you know, but who you know. Nazir, Isuru,
and I once went to a union training in northern
Minnesota. I was able to meet a number of influential
union leaders who talked about their experiences
organizing. I remember meeting the president of the
nurse's union. Isuru jokingly mentioned that I might
run for office and, to my shock, she took it seriously.
She asked me a number of questions related to my

background and organizing work. I was flattered but insisted that I wasn't ready. She gave me some words of encouragement and told me to contact her if I ever wanted to know more about nurses. I also had a similar experience when attending a union contract bargaining with Nazir. I got to see firsthand janitors unite to negotiate a contract with their employers. During the lunch break, Nazir and the lawyer representing the big corporations were late to get into the line for lunch. The lawyer commented, "Slim pickings, aye?" in an effort to create small talk. Nazir wittingly and comically replied, "I thought you were getting seconds." expressing disdain for his greed during negotiations. The lawyer replied with a conciliatory "no" and proceeded to grab his lunch. After a day of unsuccessful negotiations, the mood of the workers was jubilant. The idea that merely amalgamating and demanding better conditions was enough to toot their horns. Nazir brought me up to one of the leading organizers and introduced the two of us. The man was very impressed by my age and expressed his appreciation for my attendance on a school day. I thanked him for the opportunity to witness such an uplifting process and wished him luck in future negotiations.

He gave me his contact information and asked me to stay in touch. For networking to work, both sides need to be willing to keep in contact with each other. I believe that one thing that is advantageous for young people in today's world is the ability to find professionals willing to teach a craft or system. Obviously, I'm not implying that every kid has ample opportunity regardless of zip code or identity. It's a privilege to be able to network and I want to make that clear. I believe that there is an innate responsibility that most American adults feel to onboard the next generation. If you're persistent enough with your request, if you're articulate enough with your goal, and if you're disciplined enough with your routine, then I do not doubt that there's a connection willing to do work with you. Another successful component of networking is maintaining the relationships you build. I have never made a genuine connection I couldn't keep up with. It would make for quite an awkward situation if people utilized connections once or twice a year without proper relationship building. As Nazir and I traveled throughout the organizing scene in Minnesota, more connections were made and more lessons were learned. Another common activity Nazir and I explored was the protest scene, particularly in Minneapolis & Saint Paul. As we were about to leave for one of our meetups, we noticed a journalist questioning an elder. It was abnormal for journalists to be in this particular part of town, so we got a little closer to try to decipher what the interview had been about. The interviewer was asking far-right rhetorical and loaded questions, capitalizing on the fact that the elder didn't speak English as well. Nazir and I got out of the car to question the journalist, only to find out that he belonged to a right-wing media outlet based in Canada. After applying verbal pressure for a lack of fair and accurate journalism on his part, he eventually capitulated and left. Perhaps the biggest protest that involved my friend group was the season-long protest that stemmed from the murder of George Floyd. Nazir was in New York, but I spent most of those days with Bol, Jacob, and a friend named Wako. Nazir and I would regularly check in about what the current situation was in Minneapolis and eventually the situation in New York City as the protests spread across the country faster than a wildfire. I plan to dedicate a larger portion of this particular period in the last chapter. During one of the nights, there was a group of individuals who attacked the small business under my condominium. The idea that a fire could be lit was terrifying and well-warranted, so I called in some resources that had been offered by ordinary folks patrolling the city in an effort to ward off these individuals in the absence of police. I remember reaching out to Nazir all the way in New York. He was connected with the situation on the ground in Minneapolis and instantly sent resources to aid. The groups of individuals came in different increments, so no one knew when the next wave would show up. As an hour passed by another car filled with occupants pulled up with visible baseball bats in their hands. I braced myself for the worst and encouraged my neighbors to take off because if an altercation ensued, we were understaffed and unprepared to defend the property and residents. As the individuals came out of the car and their shadows slowly crept closer, I could feel my heart racing at the sound of feet shuffling on the other side of the street. I stared down at one of the men, desperately trying to identify him. I then noticed a hair pattern that peculiarly fit Jacob's style and then heard Bol's friendly voice. I instantly threw my hands up in grace screaming "Bol!" "Jacob!" "Wako!" and assured the neighbors that these were my friends and they were here to help. Wako and his sister accompanied them and stood in front of the businesses all night, ensuring that another break-in wouldn't occur. My friends had my back through some of the most uncertain tumultuous times. I cannot express how grateful I am to Nazir for orchestrating the rescue. In life, you always hear advice about friendship; who you should and shouldn't surround yourself with. To truly understand how difficult it was to show up that night. I'll conclude with the statement that if your friends rush to your aid during a doomsday scenario, then you've got the right friends. During one of the nights, Jacob, Wako, and I were out doing community defense, a term coined during the uprising that followed the murder of George Floyd. Folks who took part in community defense were everyday citizens wanting to help in the absence of police. We were driving on the other side of town when we quickly realized that access points into different places throughout the city had been blocked by the national guard. While we were driving to our location, two minutes had passed the curfew, imposed by the governor, so everyone was feeling nervous about what the response may be by authorities. We had to continuously change routes because of the many national guard blockades. As we finally found a route that was clear, we were quickly met by a massive contingent of humvees to our left side, and then unexpectedly again, a massive contingent of armored vehicles followed by several other kinds of military vehicles on our right side. It became clear that we had found a military transportation route, and it became even more clear that we were in serious jeopardy of being stopped. Luckily, we slowed down our speed and the national guard smoothly passed by. Wako, who was the driver, expressed his wariness about driving back home later, so we went looking for a place to crash for the night. Isuru didn't live too far and offered to host us. We gladly accepted. After what seemed like an eternity, we finally got to Isuru's house, where we spent a good portion of the night discussing the current situation. Wako joined a community defense contingent a block or two away, leaving Isuru, Jacob, and me to discuss. The primary concern for everyone was the difficulty of turning the energy in the streets into a sustainable, successful movement. We all witnessed the explosive combustion of anger from the community and felt a sense of liberation and sadness. We also knew that for it to mean anything, there needed to be coordinated pressure applied on many fronts. Bol had fallen at one of the protests, but the extent of his injuries was unknown to me until he later displayed both of his forearms in casts. He fractured both of his forearms. I assumed he didn't join us for community defense because he was feeling sore, but I was shocked to hear the extent of his injuries. An injury we all experienced was the temporary burning sensation of being tear-gassed. Due to the massive numbers of people, police were brutally and indiscriminately throwing what seemed to be unlimited rounds of tear gas on civilians. I was fortunate enough to never directly get hit with tear gas, but I accidentally ran into its fumes plenty of times. The fumes were enough to get me coughing, to temporarily blind me, and to mentally agitate me. I was also hit by a piece of shrapnel from a rubber bullet in my abdomen. Bol shared that he was warning people to retreat from the site when two canisters of rubber bullets were thrown a couple of feet in front of him. As he ran away from the canisters, he was surprised by a fence. As the tall person he is, jumping wasn't the only way to get over it, so as he attempted to hop over the fence and was unsuccessful, which ultimately led to him falling and fracturing his fore-arms. Jacob also caught some fumes, but Isuru was able to dodge the worst effects because of his already cautious social distancing habits. He was able to stay a significant distance away from the massive crowds. Tear gas spreads long distances, and it stays in the air for a while, so he too was affected. Nazir, staying in the heart of New York City, routinely had to deal with tear gas seeping into his home. If there is one thing we all took away from this experience, it was to always come prepared for protests. Even though the experience felt isolating at times, I truly believe that it brought us all closer together. A tragedy occurred, and it was almost like everyone felt the same level of frustration and pain. Instead of retreating into our respective corners and torturing our minds with the words "I can't breathe" over and over, we mentally connected to create a cathartic experience. The action that occurred in the streets was exciting, but the ideas on how to move forward were just as stimulating. When Nazir came back from New York, we both exchanged stories about our concurrent experiences during the protests. I clowned him by saying that the only reason he came back so soon was because of FOMO. He reluctantly conceded by stating that it was good to be home. One of the most notable things Nazir instilled in me is the ability to be humble. He didn't teach me this lesson by telling me to be humble or by crushing my ego verbally. He instead led by example. Nazir's lifestyle is one of a humble man. From living in a modest apartment in south Minneapolis to spending hours working to create an environmentally sustainable earth. He not only talks the talk but walks the walk; his vast collection of succulents serve as a piece of evidence. One of the many conversations I can recall we had on this topic was coming back from an organizing event. Nazir was driving me home while I was sitting in the shotgun talking up a storm per usual. At the event, I had an interaction with an individual who previously knew me. They were rude and made a particular snarky comment that I found to be offensive. I smiled and played it off, but after, I vented about how awful the situation was. Nazir listened and concurred with my analysis of the inappropriate behavior coming from the individual. I then berated the integrity of the individual to further vent my frustration. Nazir could have agreed and added fuel to the flames by saying more things I wanted to hear, but he instead offered some good advice. He said that the individual's mistreatment of me was indicative of their confidence, or lack thereof. He mentioned that I knew how talented I was and others realized it as well, but it would be foolish to think that everyone would react in a positive way. I sat on that for a while during the ride home. I thought to myself, why stoop to a level so low and give that person the power to frustrate me? I agreed but said that it would be hard for me to forgive, let alone forget, the disrespect. He then replied with something so eye-opening, "That's understandable but if that's all you choose to remember, then you will never forget." I questioned what that meant and got a detailed explanation. He explained the fact that we decided to go to this event for a reason unrelated to the incident that occurred. Even though that incident took up a small amount of time, it ended up tainting the positive takeaways overall. I chose to focus on that little piece of negativity while ignoring the overwhelming pieces of positivity. After later analysis, I began to see how big of a pattern it was in my life and in the lives of so many people. We don't do it because negativity is innately more flamboyant or powerful.

We do it because we are subconsciously programmed to search for those tendencies and hash them out over and over again, tainting our overall attitude. Nazir then told me to close my eyes. I reluctantly closed my eyes. He told me to open my eyes and point out everything blue within a ten-second frame; he'd question me after based on my recollection. I opened them and pointed out a number of things, starting with the sky. After ten seconds, he told me to close my eyes again. He then asked me to recall everything I remember seeing with the color red. I laughed and said, "You mean blue." He said, "no, red." I froze. Once I spent a bit of time trying to recall one object with the color red, he gave an explanation for the exercise. "If we choose to view the world through one color, then we will miss out on all the other colors." he then concluded with this analogy: "When we view detailed paintings, we expect to see many colors because that's the point of paintings, so why would we expect to live our detailed lives through one color?" I remember feeling a sense of enlightenment and courage after hearing that. It was a lesson in maturity, but it was also a lesson in humbleness. A humble person always keeps an open mind. By expecting everyone to appreciate you, or in the least treat you with respect, are signs of an inflated ego. Understanding that you cannot control how people feel about you and that no one is immune to criticism or disrespect are signs of humbleness. You don't and shouldn't have to accept disrespect, but you also shouldn't let it catch you off guard. It should be expected and dealt with in a healthy manner. Throughout the chapter, I've discussed the impact that a man named Nazir had on me, and the many great people he has brought into my life. Although I can't tout a record of knowing him for decades, I can undoubtedly say that there will be decades to come. From our countless mini road trips to the many gatherings we've had with friends, I know that the road we have yet to travel eclipses the paths we have already crossed. Our relationship goes past mentor and mentee. Our relationship takes on a mold of an older and younger brother. That definition would have to expand to include Isuru, Bol, Jacob, Wako, and Kong. We're all brothers untied through a common struggle. I've shared this earlier in the chapter, but I feel it's important to restate how lucky I was to have met this group at this stage in my life. If you surround yourself with great people, you will live a great life, and what else can one ask for? As a young person, it's critical that you have the right influences in your life because of the lack of life experience you have and your ability to create positive social habits. You don't have to find an older group of friends like I did, but checking in with someone who's got a little more experience in this game we call life isn't such a bad idea. This also applies to adults because many of our elders reign supreme in the realm of wisdom. They say home is where your heart is and I've found a home in Nazir, Isuru, Bol, Kong, Wako, and Jacob. They've stuck by me through hard times and they've celebrated with me during the good times. They truly are my brothers for life.

Chapter 4:

C Student

Talented mediocrity at its finest.

I BELIEVE THAT THE TRUE measure of one's intelligence depends on how one distributes their time on any given craft. Some people can excel in many disciplines, others not so much. Our schooling system attempts to force a flawed understanding of knowledge onto the masses. Our children undergo a rigorous amount of coursework and are expected to reach fluency in each subject. If a student is an amazing mathematician yet cannot understand the motives behind Shakespeare, then they're at risk of not graduating. The insane part about this system is we do not expect our children to comprehend this information long term, yet we feed it to them guilt-free. I think every child should be able to read at an appropriate reading level and I believe that every child should be able to conduct a basic level of arithmetic because these tasks are undergone on a daily basis. We insist on forcing advanced algebra and chemistry down our children's throats without giving them the option to opt-out. If a child dares to question whether or not the information being fed into them will be pertinent in several years, we shut them down. If I had a dime for every time I heard a teacher say "You may need it when you get older." or "This is something you will use every day." after being questioned, I would have enough money to pay for a student's college tuition. I know teachers have limited flexibility when it comes to the overall teaching curriculum, but there needs to be more push back from teachers' unions on this front. When kids lose interest in school, they usually only lose interest in one or two subjects. The problem with school is that it's a package deal; meaning you must do well in everything or it doesn't count. This ultimatum often leaves students feeling like they're dumb. It prohibits them from excelling in other fields long term. The mental anchor of failing a class or two is taxing. Shame on us. I remember showing my first strengths and weaknesses back in third grade. I loved geography and literature; I was liberal arts minded, however, I didn't do too well with math. The emphasis the adults in my life put on excelling at math took its toll on my academic confidence. Now, I wasn't dangerously behind in the subject, but I was bad enough to where I lost interest in it. I was the most advanced student regarding oration and geography. For some reason, my excelling in those subjects wasn't as valuable as me excelling in math. There was a gifted and talented program at our school and its presence was well felt. In order to qualify for the program, you had to be an advanced mathematician. I remember feeling a sense of inferiority sink in each time I read over my report card, and seeing the column for "Gifted & Talented" with an N/A for not assessed next to it. Not every school values math over the liberal arts, but the entire system looks to create a false meritocracy. Then you've got the issue of testing. We over-test our students. The problem with testing today is it confines our country's potential to a simple multiple-choice question. It forces teachers to teach to a test rather than to the real world. We have valued test results over our student's mental health. Where are America's most established institutions on this? Harvard, Yale, Princeton, Dartmouth, and every Ivy League has emphasized the importance of testing. You cannot expect to get into an Ivy League without a good ACT or SAT score. This requirement puts so much strain on the students of America. I remember sitting in my school's gymnasium the day we took one of the national standardized tests. I saw some of my peers show up at school with bags under their eyes because they'd been studying all night. I could feel this tension and fear arise from everyone sitting down, worried about their future. There is so much emphasis put on getting a high score that students usually plan their future based on their score alone. I showed up with some nerves because of hearing about the importance of the test since I was a kindergartner. The nerves were put to rest as I began to see how much more nervous others were. There is something about dealing with a shared feeling or reaction that makes it more tolerable to deal with. I was less mesmerized by the idea of getting a high score and more mesmerized by seeing all of my peers in one place working on the same problems. I then had the idea that if we're all working on the same problems, why not solve them together? What a radical idea, huh? We've become so accustomed to individualism that we've failed to use one of our greatest strengths, which is unity. As individuals, there is only so much we can do, but together, the possibilities are endless. I think entire senior classes should take the test as a cohesive whole. Instead of having a short-term impact on students; merely for admission purposes. The test would have a fundamental lifelong impact on our students, teaching them a set of strong characteristic traits, strong communication skills, and an appreciation of their own strengths and weaknesses alongside others. This will probably never happen because, in order for our children to be set up to succeed in such a way; we would need to reboot our curriculum and teaching methods. In the essay portion of the test — the final stage — we were given a writing prompt. I used that opportunity to send a message to the powers that be. I wrote about how irresponsible it was to assign a "one size fits all" test to a diverse group of strengths and weaknesses. I talked about the outdatedness of the test alongside its

poor academic rigor assessment. I concluded by pro-
claiming my independence from a blatantly insulting
indoctrination attempt. After submitting the test, on
my way out, one of the staff members asked me how
I felt about the difficulty of the last portion. With a
smile on my face, I sighed and said, "I could have done
it in my sleep." The truth of the matter is that this test
only took up a minute fraction of my overall academic
career. My reaction didn't come from out of the blue,
but had been the culmination of my thoughts and
experiences leading up to it. From kindergarten
through fifth grade, I was graded through a compli-
cated system of ones and fours. Whenever report
cards were issued, there would be about twenty col-
umns with numbers ranging from one through four;
one being dissatisfactory and four being advanced.
This system assessed students not on work being
turned in, but on the teacher's presumption of where
a student's skills were at. As some of you may have
assumed, I received ones and twos, with the occasional three in writing and communication. It wasn't
until writing this section of the book that I could fully
conceive how flawed the system was in its entirety.
When one teacher is tasked with keeping multiple

mental tabs on a classroom, usually ranging anywhere from eighteen to twenty-four students, then regardless of who the teacher is; the results will come out inaccurate to a noticeable degree. The anxiety that I felt before every report card was sent out is unmatched to this day. The usual way these things would work would be for me to find out from a classmate that their report cards were finally mailed out. I would then get picked up and brought home to an open report card on the living room table. Not much was said for a couple of days, but the gesture itself spoke louder than any words ever could. In middle school, I was finally introduced to the regular letter grading system. With the letter grading system, I became more cognizant of my strengths and weaknesses. I was slowly solidifying my status as a "C" student. It's one thing for a student to receive low to mediocre grades after struggling with the rigor. It's another thing for a student to not put in the effort. In some cases, academic rigor can be overwhelming for a student, so the student decides to completely check out; the same situation can happen in reverse where the rigor is too easy. For me, it was both. Mathematics was too difficult, so I avoided it altogether. History, English, and Government rigor was way too easy, leaving me no choice but to spend my time studying more advanced topics in those subjects. In eighth grade, I was struck with a sensory overload due to all the hype around the 2016 presidential election. The most intriguing part for me was the democratic primary. I made a bet with my teacher over a sandwich that Bernie Sanders would win the primary. Although the outcome didn't end in my favor, I was hooked, and for the first time since beginning my chess career; I had a new hobby. At the beginning of high school, the idea of getting into Harvard University was appealing. I finished my freshman year with a "B" average, but finished high school with an overall "C" average. This was troubling for the adults tracking my academic progress. I had grown so much as a person throughout my four years in high school and I developed leadership skills that were invaluable to my success outside school. If there was ever an example of grades not reflecting a student's capabilities, then I was the prime example. I felt annoyed whenever a teacher had their laptop open during one of the many staff meetings I was invited to. I worried they would be so impressed with my developed and well-articulated opinions they would want to check my GPA — I didn't want to disappoint. My mother and older brother accepted the evidence and concluded that school wasn't for me. They weren't too worried about it because of my extra-curricular activities, but they would constantly remind me of the importance of attaining "the paper" as an economic safety net. My younger sister was a polar opposite student compared to me. She would attain high academic marks like it was second nature. When describing her achievements, I would always say that "academia is her playground." My mother could seek solace in knowing that she had at least one child she could rely on to bring home straight A's. I believe that students who get high marks in school are intelligent and disciplined. I want to clarify that my criticism of school doesn't coincide with my opinion of people who excel in it. After all, it's a game and sometimes you've got to play the game in order to get what you want. If you ask a majority of straight "A" students whether they are in love with the bulk of the curriculum, they excel at you'll probably hear more of a negative response. Proponents of school will argue that schooling instills a degree of tenacity in students, which is undoubtedly a life skill one needs to survive in the real world. I do not believe that the issue is about 'toughening up' our kids. If that were the case, we would have rectified the cracks that many of our kids are falling through. Why would we intentionally set our kids up to fail without providing a safety net for them to rely on? This would be akin to sending navy seals into training underwater, without an instructor present to monitor their oxygen. Or doing test crashes with actual humans in the cars instead of manikins. Those examples weren't exaggerations. Students are literally failing in mass numbers and there aren't any meaningful solutions being implemented to save them. When a majority of kids fail in school, the impact that has on their lives can be calamitous. From the school-to-prison pipeline to difficulty finding employment in an increasingly competitive job market. We all will indirectly feel the effects of this. If it isn't to 'toughen up' our students, then why do we continue to support this outdated system? The only benefit that I can see is profit. The reason it's harder to find the profit motive is because there isn't a single entity responsible for retaining it, it's a team effort. First, you have the owners of the for-profit industrial prison complex who build prisons based on the reading tests of third-grade students. They're relying on a certain demographic to fill their prisons, so they need to monitor future profit. Then you have the politicians at both the state and national level that love to gut funds for educating our kids, so that they can either fund other programs or give tax breaks to the wealthy. Then you've got industries that need low-paying workers so they have some interest in controlling how the next batch comes out. I think the biggest influence corporations have had on our schools relates to the culture. Students have to ask for permission to use the bathroom, to use a water fountain, and, are expected to show up very early in the morning. Finally, it's our standardized test and university system. There is broad consensus that standardized tests do more harm than good, yet year after year schools open their doors to them. Then our university system comes in and requires high marks on tests for admission, which forces schools to teach to the test. They also make their institutions extremely expensive, adding guaranteed economic strain with a mix of false hope. This major conglomerate works against the best interest of our students and there isn't a thing they can do about it. Who will stand up for our students? Whenever they themselves say anything, they're instantly silenced and labeled as naïve or lazy. If a teacher stands up, then they're at risk of being punished by the district for insubordination. Parents want the best for their kids, so they have to pick and choose their battles wisely; most are either too busy working or are uninformed about the powers that be. You definitely cannot count on politicians; many of whom are just as outdated as the system. One of the reasons that I wrote this chapter is because there needs to be more perspective coming from students who take issue with our current education system. This perspective comes from someone who wasn't necessarily a model student, but also someone who didn't completely fall through the cracks. This isn't a part of a Ph.D. student's dissertation or a governmental agency's analysis. It's an unfiltered view of a "C" student's recent history in America's public schools. Part of my disinterest in school came from the early realization of how things were operating. I didn't fall for the capitalistic pitch that sprung from CEOs dropping out to become an entrepreneur. I don't think that dropping out hoping to become a mega-billionaire was any safer. The biggest challenge I had was showing up every day and putting a smile on my face, knowing that there are a bunch of more valuable things I could be doing during school days. This mantra of stoicism was tested especially hard during my senior year of high school. I had my license, and I had more than enough credits to graduate. My schedule was one every student dreamed of. I was what the school called an "aide" for a teacher during my first hour. An aide pretty much sits around and helps a teacher with whatever they need. Since the teacher I was aiding for didn't have a class during the first hour of the school day, I pretty much just sat around and either used my phone or participated in political conversations with said teacher. The teacher's name was Corbin. He was and still is an exceptional educator. I took a class of his during my freshman year and we kept in contact, mainly through occasional run-ins in the hallway. I learned so much from my conversations with him during my senior year that learning became fun. I would wake up and try to get to school on time to maximize the length our conversations would take up. It's rare for students to make an extra effort to get to school on time, especially in their senior year of high school. I mentioned to Corbin on numerous occasions that aiding for him was one of the most educational experiences I'd undertaken, highlighting the fruitfulness of our time spent together. He would always grin and comment, "You're just saying that to pass," attempting to hide his jubilation. I could tell he was flattered to hear it. After spending some time with Corbin, I'd got to visit Alex, the Equity & Diversity Coordinator. Alex and I would have the deepest conversations about personal and academic life. I learned a lot of organizing principles from him. On the days I wouldn't make it to his office due to being busy, I'd eventually catch up to him and jokingly say, "Still trying to avoid me, aye?" I learned through these experiences the importance of having the right educators in our schools. The right educator will have the ability to change a student's life. The right educator will also give the student(s) an opportunity to change his or her life. After my daily check-ins/talks with Corbin and Alex, the incentive to stay in school for the rest of the day drastically diminished. I stacked my schedule with electives, so 70% of my day was packed with keep-busy work. The number one battle a student in my position faced wasn't tackling challenging academic rigor. It was maintaining attendance. For the first time in my academic career, my

GPA wasn't my Achilles Heel. This was a challenge many of my peers in the same grade faced. It's almost as if we were developmentally done and the system was also done with us, but archaic cultural standards held us back. The notion that seniors "run" the school comes from a lack of things for them to do. Many seniors in high school across America roam their halls with nothing to do waiting for the end of the school year so that they can finally move on with life. All the absences that were pitted against me taught me a valuable skill. I learned the power of negotiation. This art is thought to be dictated by the basic fundamental principles that make up a meritocracy. We're taught that if one side comes out with more during negotiations, then they were just better at negotiating. There is a critical element that must be considered before the negotiations start. That critical element is the assessment of negotiating power that both sides bring to the table. One often thinks that the decision-making gets done at the negotiating table, when, in actuality, the result has already been determined before both sides have taken their seats. Once this is understood at the national level, we'll be able to slowly dissect our false meritocracy model; which creates fairness in all of our sectors. I mentioned a portion of my views towards negotiations on a macro level because there are parallels that I came to realize with negotiations on a micro-level. For example, the negotiating power between a student and a teacher is disproportionate. The teacher is in a position of immense power over the student(s) and in the vast majority of cases, they have the final say over the outcome. The student has several choices to increase their negotiating power, ensuring a fair process. They can either individually appeal to a teacher's decision in the hopes that the teacher will find their self-advocacy admirable, or they can rally up some of their peers and attempt to appeal to their teacher's democratic values. They can go to a school administrator in an attempt to have the top nachos intervene, kind of like how the Supreme Court may intervene in a decision made by a lower court. They can go to their parents in what I think is one of the most effective tools to use, especially at the lower grade levels. There is a plethora of options if students are willing to strategize. I learned that a portion of my grade would be determined by my negotiating skills because of my natural lethargy towards schoolwork and the absences that stacked up.

Although I must admit, my negotiating skills were perfected throughout my entire schooling career; pinpointing each exercise would require a time machine and a mind reader. The parallels become evident when adults share stories about not being able to afford their prescription drugs or not being able to pay off their mounting student loan debt. Our system conditions people to accept an inferior status whenever one is pitted up against the system, but it also does something else. For those who continue to push and strategize, there is a striking realization. Individually, we bear little to no negotiating power, but as a unified whole, there is no telling what we can accomplish. The negotiating strength of a unified pack is stronger than the negotiating strength of one individual tenfold. The reason I continue to bring up negotiating in a chapter titled "C" student is because if there is one thing students in this academic group share, it's the understanding of how important this skill is. Every "C" student earned their grade because they failed to negotiate a better grade or because they successfully negotiated a better grade. There are a handful of kids who literally strive for academic mediocrity, but the vast majority either shoot for the stars or slack off. One

would ask, if "C" students are so familiar with negotiating, then why can't they negotiate a better grade?
The answer is complex. I've found that one of the most
crippling factors to any student's success is procrastination. If one develops a habit of severe procrastination, then there isn't any amount of negotiations that'll
cover for a continued lack of quality in work. There is
also a fair share of students that wouldn't bother to
negotiate a higher grade simply because a "C" would
suffice. I would have considered myself to be a part of
that group of students. My aim isn't to romanticize
getting a "C" or the individual who constantly achieves
it. My objective is to showcase how an advanced skill
can be perfected through a mediocre grade. I think I
was unbothered by my academic standing because of
the amount of extra-curricular activities that I had
going on for me. This illustrates a skill that I had that
students in all grade categories can develop. That skill
is called self-confidence. I've noticed that students
with the highest marks usually have the lowest levels
of self-confidence. This is shown through a number
of habits; constantly second guessing themselves
because of what's on the line, anti-socialness due to
being book worms, constant pressure from parents to

excel, etc. You've always got the one kid who happens to be president of every club and who holds bilateral conversations with the school's administration once every week. This student may appear to be self confident, but they usually end up being the most self-conscious. It screams through their need to excel at everything. The students who end up failing are usually the most self-confident. This is because they've mastered the art of being social. They're too social for their own good. They end up sacrificing their academic potential for social clout that usually ends up being temporary. Then you've got the "C" Students who tend to be both academically confident and socially confident. They're usually oozing with self-confidence. In my case, I was confident enough to share my GPA with others even if they'd question my intelligence after. I never felt the need to prove myself; not to colleges, not to my peers, not to my parent, not to my teachers — not to anyone. My parent would occasionally ponder the idea of me trying harder simply because a prestigious university is an option I may want to explore later, but I insisted that I wasn't going to be interested in wining and dining with the elites. Some of my teachers weren't surprised and explained that GPA wasn't an indicator of intelligence, let alone academic potential. There wasn't an overall theme or reaction that came from people's responses, and I think folks instead were more inclined to question the validity of our grading system. I wouldn't go back and tell myself to get higher marks. I would encourage myself to continue to have confidence in the hobbies I developed and to continue to participate in the extracurricular activities that I was doing. I'd like for readers to seriously question the use of our grading system. Why do we grade our students like they're products at a supermarket? Generation after generation, there are people who reach the pinnacles of financial and social success who defy the academic odds. Even though the chorus of parents, teachers and students grow louder and louder in the name of reform, our grading system seems to grow in importance. The collateral price is being paid through the mental health of our students. 44% of college students reported being depressed and the number of high schools students who feel that way is probably higher. Sadly, the false narrative of incrementalism has plagued our institutions of higher learning just as they've plagued our institutions of healthcare and criminal justice. Teachers answer to the principal and the principal answers to the school board, and the school board answers to the state, and the state answers to the federal government through the Department of Education, who in turn answers to Congress and the President. In a sense, this chain of command ensures the continuity of policies throughout the entire country, but the issue is that there isn't a clear way to overhaul those policies. Gridlock in Washington backs up everything. Instead of implementing timely reforms, parents, students, and teachers are forced to accept the rhetoric of lukewarm acceptance; keyword: rhetoric — no action. So, is there any hope for our children? Yes! Sure, our teachers are underpaid and our children are depressed, but on the bright side there's an abundance of antiquated textbooks sitting in classrooms all over the country! That means there can be no shortage in supply. In all seriousness, though, I worry about our country's future. America's schools aren't living up to their fullest potential. This will continue to have a domino effect on other vital sectors and industries in our country. As we continue to move away from a warehouse economy, the need for ingenuity has only grown. The shortage in STEM graduates has forced us to look elsewhere for high-paying skilled labor. The digital technology sector has seen the most growth over the past several decades, but our curriculum does not reflect the preparation that should be in order for our children. We're not going to be able to out-man the rising economies in China and India, so we ought to stick to what made us number one in the first place; creativity. If we're going to retain that creativity, we're going to need to start funneling it towards our education system. The people who will have the biggest impact on reforming the system aren't the people who enjoy excelling in it. Believe it or not, the kid who spends most of his time doodling in math class may go on to be one of the world's best problem solvers. Ultimately, that's what this chapter is all about. Not every "C" student shares the same views of the world, or even of the education system as me — hell, not every "C" student wants to receive the marks they get, but the fact remains that the stigma around being "mediocre" or "average" is far from the truth. Students who receive those marks are often amongst some of the brightest in the classroom. It seems as though "C" students are often overlooked. "A" students are usually a part of an advanced scholar program, and the students who are flunking usually are the focus points for the school. Through rhetoric or resources. In my opinion, the question isn't whether we'll have the courage to take a bold stance on how we choose to educate our children; the question is when? How many more generations must wait for common sense reform? I remain optimistic about my generation's ability to change things. After all, we're the generation of updates. We've become accustomed to change. Sooner or later, the spirit of something new will affect our learning institutions for the better.

Chapter 5:

Green New Deal

A Taste.

I 'VE ALWAYS HEARD OF the revolutionary "New Deal" throughout my schooling, but it wasn't until the later years of my youth that I came to fully appreciate its significance. Franklin Delano Roosevelt, a boy of privilege, grew up in a world where wealth wasn't a dream but an early morning reality. Perhaps one of the reasons I felt that The New Deal was so significant is because of the chief architect behind it. In the midst of the Great Depression, Roosevelt witnessed that workers were consistently getting the short end of the stick; offering them a new deal. This plan would go on to become one of the strongest pieces of positive change sent from Washington to the everyday worker. This was done at one of the country's lowest points. You're probably asking yourself, what significance does this piece of legislation that was enacted nearly a hundred years ago have to this chapter? Well, you'd have to look to Alexandria Ocasio-Cortez. Like in the 1930s, our country is facing a crisis that incrementalism won't solve — let alone slow down. The climate crisis can only be met through an international effort of radical reform. Alexandria recognized the need for bold climate legislation, so she coined the "New Deal" adding a twist, naming it the "Green New Deal". Although its chance of passing in Congress was slim to none, the statement it sent electrified the left. In no time, Green New Deal bills were popping up in legislatures across the country. In Minnesota, things were a little different. Instead of having a bill carried by politicians, it was carried by youth. It was called the MN Green New Deal. I ended up going to an environmental event in my neighborhood where I met a group of folks who were connected to this piece of legislation. It was in its infant stages when I was first introduced to it. This was in my junior year of high school, so I had built some awareness around climate policy. The first draft of the bill had already been written by a small group of students from the suburbs. This group of students formed an organization called MN Can't Wait. It was advised and supported by various adults in the environmental community. When I first arrived on the scene, my rhetorical skills were quickly noted by the youth and adults I was working with. A major press conference was planned to announce the bill's introduction. I wasn't originally chosen to speak, but when one of the youth speakers got cold feet; the opportunity presented itself, so I took it. Now, until this point, I'd never done much public speaking — let alone in a press conference setting. I remember writing my speech and practicing it in the mirror, ignoring the thought of flopping. On the day of the press conference, I left school early, stopped by my house to put on the proper attire, and hopped in my mother's car to head straight to the MN State Capitol where the press conference would be held. By this time, my nerves had turned into an overall sensation of numbness. As I entered the Capitol, I was met by a team of

PR specialists who gave me a pep talk and advice on how to conduct myself at the podium. To my side was a young woman whom I'd befriended throughout the process of writing the bill. We had coordinated some of our remarks before, but we didn't take the time to build speaking chemistry — that wouldn't be an issue. Right before the press conference began, large swaths of journalists entered the room while a group of politicians and nonprofit leaders gathered behind the podium. One of the main areas that people look at during a press conference is behind the speaker. Many folks don't realize this until they've participated in a press conference, but you have to be cognizant of how you present yourself throughout the entire ordeal. When you're standing behind someone at a podium, you've got to keep your gaze on the back of their head or the center of their back. You'll also naturally drift away and look into the crowd of people in the room, but it's important to not drift away for too long because then you'll look lost. Facial expressions are also important because it shows your listening, and that you care. Obviously, everything has a limit, so don't overdo it. When I was standing up there for the first time, these rules came naturally to me. Maybe it was from all the political press conferences I'd been watching. During the press conference, I thought to myself, how could there be any sensible opposition to this bill? There were faith leaders, scientists, and youth advocating for something that would save everyone from catastrophe. I was moved by the dedication stakeholders showed and the amount of attention it was getting in the press. When it was my turn to speak, I went along with energy present in the room. After I finished my remarks, the room lit up in applause — something I wasn't expecting. It wasn't until I got home and watched the press conference that I realized how well I did. It was in reviewing that press conference that I thought to myself, hmm… I could do this. An adroit politician can articulate a solution to a problem that affects so many. A great politician is able to create passion where there is indifference. In order to be a great politician, one must truly believe in what they are doing. I think I was able to articulate the need for unity around the "MN Green New Deal" because I truly cared about it; after all, I wrote a portion of it. I, alongside many of the youth, thought that there was enough external pressure to get the bill passed. That prospect fueled my passion and motivation. There were some Republican legislators who met with and acknowledged our cries for change. I remember sitting on a panel with a Republican legislator from a small town in rural Minnesota. He talked about how much of his district has already switched their reliance from fossil fuels to environmentally friendly energy resources. His main issue was that the party leader wouldn't allow him to cast a vote in favor of renewable resources; let alone a "Green New Deal". This is where politics fails to rise to the moment. When special interests usurp the role of the public interest, then chaos ensues. The reason special interests are able to take a front-row seat with regard to the issues being discussed is that they use politicians to manipulate the public into thinking that their interests are aligned with the public. Almost every Republican legislator I spoke with behind closed doors was on board with the idea of getting ahead of this issue. They were willing to forget about the promises they made in the previous election and instead were focused on re-election. I sought counsel with a senior democratic legislator because I was perplexed by how entangled the process of passing this bill was beginning to be. He sat me down in his office and looked me in my eye — as if he'd explained what he was about to say a million times before. "Here in the legislature you vote one of three ways; you either vote with your caucus, your conscience, or your constituency. In that order." One would think that since you only get to choose one, you'll eventually be forced to vote against your interests. Most of the time, all three align, so it isn't a decision that needs to be made often. The problem is when you are forced to vote with your caucus even when it goes against your conscience and your constituency. Politicians will never come out and say that they voted for a piece of legislation even though they didn't believe in it, or even though it went against the interest of their constituents, so they are forced to defend it. Deception becomes the name of the game. When politicians attempt to sell a piece of legislation to their constituents, they're not just selling that individual piece of legislation, but they're selling an entire ideology. Public opinion often ends up being skewed because of the power in an elected official's opinion. A short term strategy ends up having long-term repercussions. I was stunned and confused by the simplistic yet candid breakdown of how our state government functions. I was also disillusioned by where I was hearing it from. The legislator didn't specifically point to the Republican party when describing the system, so it was clearly prevalent throughout both parties. Both Democrats and Republicans are adherent to that mantra. After the end of my discussion with the senior democratic legislator, all I could think about was whether it was worth staying politically active. I figured that if the game was already decided before the whistle was blown, then what's the point of even playing? Climate change is no doubt the biggest challenge our species has ever faced. We brought upon this process not through the instant acceleration of harmful agents, but by the decades of inaction due to corruption. We've risen to the challenge before with regard to wars and depressions, but we've never risen to the level that this crisis requires of us. I came to the conclusion that in order to address climate change and a number of other issues, we must first fundamentally reform our government's day-to-day operations. There's no hope otherwise. Special interests used to spend millions of dollars trying to persuade politicians into their corners — they still do. Things have gotten so muddied and diluted that much of the costs of corruption are automatically offset by partisanship.

Both parties acknowledge that our government is broken, yet both fail to work together to fix it. Even when either party wins an outright majority, there is still little to no systemic reform implemented. One would think that an issue as overarching and threatening as climate change would brew enough coffee for our politicians to smell, but the special interests create a smell of oil that blinds members on both sides of the aisle. When Alexandria Ocasio-Cortez proposed the "Green New Deal," we were finally given a comprehensive solution to the problem of climate change. Since certain aspects threatened the role of big oil companies in our economy, an entire party weaponized oil against its own citizens. Not supporting oil was equivalent to not supporting America's economic prosperity, or not supporting minors as they work to feed their families. If you supported this piece of legislation, then you were deemed too radical and unpatriotic by Republicans. When Republicans started attacking the "Green New Deal" they were altering millions of American's minds on environmental sustainability. This attitude trickled down from Washington to state legislatures all across the country. It didn't matter how many rallies we held, how many town halls we held, or how many private meetings we held; the majority of Republican legislators had already made up their minds. Perhaps the biggest gut punch was that the Majority Leader of the Minnesota state senate, which was a Republican, wouldn't even hold a vote on the bill. This was indicative of how much the Republican Party was consumed by special interests in the legislature. Why not hold a vote? If you felt your stance was right, then wouldn't you have wanted to vote for your conscience? If you felt that your stance was taken in the best interest of your constituents, then wouldn't you have wanted to vote for your constituency? The fact that the Majority Leader wouldn't even give his members an opportunity to record their votes in the official record entailed that corruption was at play. The one function that all Americans hold near and dear is democracy. If the vast majority of Americans saw the machinations of our government and how democracy has been replaced by dollars, then there would be a political revolution tomorrow. The reason that giant oil companies have been able to operate in the shadows is because of our flawed democratic system. Since Republicans usually find themselves winning a minority of votes, they often control government through loopholes like the electoral college and gerrymandering. If oil companies can manipulate a party's agenda to match their agenda, then they've effectively created the illusion of democracy. All of a sudden, the oil agenda becomes the people's agenda. The job creation that comes with mining oil is magnified and the existential disaster of Chernobyl or the Gulf Oil Spill become erased from the memories of the electorate. At the MN legislature, I wasn't able to gauge exactly how much big oil was meddling in the process, but I could only assume one of two things. They were very heavily invested in the process because they saw a phenomenon occurring across the country where, for the first time, a change of this magnitude was being called for with regard to the environment. This would no doubt hurt their profit and lessen their influence on the government. The other assumption was that since they already had a strong lock on our government, this radical idea proposed by youth wasn't a threat at all. The overall number of young people who showed up at the Capitol meant something. Its effects may play out long term, but nonetheless they'll play out. In retrospect, there was a period in the creation of the bill that I found to be disappointing. One of the youth who was also one of the first to come to the piece of legislation ended up skirting attempts by some other youth to include a resolution around climate refugees. The youth who created the resolution were connected to refugees, either through their parents or friends. The reasoning behind his opposition was concern that the bill wasn't going to pass. An indication of our collective naive understanding of the political process. The bill was dead on arrival, regardless of how much we toned it down. He was trying to deploy a moderate strategy in a progressive space. This quickly created a division between youth along racial and geographical lines. It was through this experience that I learned that moderates, or the concept of being moderate, are incapable of pulling together the coalition that is needed to create sustainable change. The oppressed have been lied to for so long that they now have advanced detectors that pick up strategic collateral damage. I understand the wanting to compromise, but the question then becomes; who gets to compromise? In many cases, who gets compromised? It's almost like the current understanding of political compromise does more harm than good. The bill was sent to the speaker's office without the provision of a climate refugee resolution. Once the bill was introduced, the group of youth began to break away. Quarrels were breaking out between members in our meetings. Mean-spirited texts began to fly around our virtual forums. People forgot who the real enemy was. It all traced back to the decision to silence the group of youth for strategic reasons. Some may think: That's what happens when you put kids in charge. Have the adults done any better? We were trying to operate within the adult framework of politics and we ended up getting the adult results. It should be noted that we weren't completely running things autonomously from adults. We had a couple of organizations who sent some folks to act as advisors. The adults were mainly silent during the feuds and I believe that was a testament to how heavy many of the issues that were brought up. Looking back on the whole experience, there were a number of things that I would have done differently to change the outcome, but hindsight isn't a privilege one gets when they're in the heat of the moment. Things dissipated to a point of no return and the organization "MN Can't Wait" was no more. I still kept in contact with youth from all different sides of the conflict for a period. I treasured my overall experience as a member of the organization because it taught me several things. I learned more about the political process than I would have learned from a social studies class. I learned how to be confident in my body as a public speaker through the many speeches and town halls I engaged in. I learned that negative dynamics sooner or later will always play out, regardless of which space you insert yourself into. Most importantly, I learned that being politically engaged may be an option for some, but for many, it isn't. If more Americans stayed involved in the political process, then there wouldn't need to be so much external organizing around single issues. Our government needs to be watched over like a hawk by the people who it impacts so heavily. I've come to learn that there will always be someone or something watching over our government. Is it you? After all, if you're not at the table, you're on the menu. The reason I began this chapter with "A Taste" is because that's what this experience was for me. Once you see something, it's impossible to unsee it. Once I discovered all of these machinations working above the consciousness of the public, I knew I couldn't go back to being unaware. I feel like many people are quick to convey an apathetic feeling about politics because they aren't fully aware of what's going on. The major television networks can condense a breaking story into a three minute segment, but they usually only scratch the surface of a detailed series of events. Their job is to make politics as dramatic and action packed as possible. National politics gets good coverage, and it has the least amount of reach on people's everyday lives. State and local politics, on the other hand, are a different story. The days of tuning into your daily local news station are slowly coming to an end. In the social media age, people are more inclined to get their news online, either through a short video or article. The journalistic culture of Washington trickles down into the state and local news cycles, except the efforts to make it more enjoyable aren't as strong due to the innate fragile apparatus of the local news market. When climate bills come up in state and municipal entities, they are tailored to the residents and business within a body's jurisdiction. The average voter will rely on their prior knowledge, which will most likely come from the pool of national political media. Whenever a bill at the legislative level mocks a national bill, it's bound to be polarizing. When Republicans heard the "MN Green New Deal," they took the 'Green New Deal' portion and declared it dead on arrival. I believe that if the MN Green New Deal was proposed at the state level without a national framework proposal sitting in Mitch McConnell's graveyard, it may have passed. The problem is that if the majority of Republicans aren't fully reading important pieces of legislation, then the important issues that they seek to address won't be properly addressed. There are few times in history where issues become so pressing that they must be addressed with the utmost unity. Climate change is one of them. If a national climate bill is too large of a framework to implement and if state renditions are too partisan to implement, then we're screwed. One would think. Although the energy on the inside was lethargic, the energy on the outside was a concoction of passion and urgency. In conjunction with our lobbying of legislators, we hosted several rallies that turned out hundreds. It was interesting to see the two different methods work simultaneously, but it simply wasn't enough. It felt like two different worlds co-existing. This is where the name of our government comes into play. Our system of government is a Democratic Republic. We often hear the first part of that name as the main basic function of our government, but the Republic part is just as important. In a Republic, power is given to a class of elected officials. When you have a population of over 300 million citizens, giving every single person a say in what happens on every matter isn't effective or possible. One of the major cons of our Republic is the separation that occurs between politicians and their constituents. The size of protests in America have quadrupled over the past couple of decades and the main reason for that is due to the growing distance between the elected class and the general citizenry. Elected officials have their own special healthcare, banking service, pension, clearance; it's as if they play by a completely different set of rules. Their privileges have numbed them to the day-to-day struggles of the working class. There's a reason why politicians never address their rhetoric towards the homeless. It's because they don't vote. In many cases, they can't. While engagement in our democracy is optional, abiding by the rules of our republic isn't. This understanding is important to grasp because it's at the root cause of our climate inaction. When

working-class children come out in the millions to
demand elected officials to preserve their future, it's
cute. When a dozen CEOs for giant oil companies
schedule a closed door meeting, it's consequential. We
are apathetic to the struggles of those in different
socioeconomic classes because we believe that the
system isn't directly threatening our socioeconomic
standing. What we cannot realize at the moment is
that the system is multitasking in its subjugation of
lower classes. By the time it becomes evident, we're
already entrenched in a battle and distracted by the
cause. The only thing standing in the way of politicians and their constituents are marble walls. It's
extremely frustrating to see mass dissidence on one
side, and mass lethargy on the other side. The only
solution is a revolution. Activists must run for office
in droves, and they must do it at the same time. The
reason for running at the same time is that if one or
two activists get elected, then they'll constantly be
fighting off the party establishment and will find
themselves outnumbered and defeated. If a large
enough group of deeply rooted activists run and win
their races for national office, then the establishment
will be forced to capitulate. The establishment may

even cease to exist if leadership loses primaries. I think that there is a rightly felt anger among activists towards electoral politics, but the reaction of shunning out the entire process is misplaced. Although the rhetoric from neo-conservative activists is deeply concerning, there is common ground in relation to evening out the playing field in terms of representation. Rep. Ro Khanna, a Democrat from California and Rep. Matt Gaetz, a Republican from Florida, couldn't be more ideologically apart. They represent two different constituencies from two different parts of the country, but they co-sponsored a bill which would effectively get big money out of politics. Ro is a progressive so his support for this piece of legislation is a no brainer but the fact that Matt Gaetz, a rising voice in conservative politics signed on, shows that activists on both sides of the aisle share a sense of disillusionment in our government. Money creates a new motive. Half of our politicians are corrupt, and the other half is forced to navigate through the corruption behind closed doors. Why some politicians aren't transparent about the specific methods and the specific elected officials engaging in this corruption is something I have yet to wrap my mind around. One thing is

certain, I'd rather deal with a Republican who is passionate about his or her outrageous views than a sly
careerist who works for the green. I learned that there
are two spheres that never seem to effectively collide.
It is akin to the invisible line that separates the Atlantic
and Pacific oceans. In one sphere there're protests,
trends, people, and energy. In the other sphere, there's
money, power, figures, and lethargy. Both spheres try
to utilize certain aspects of the other, but for the most
part, the structures remain unrevised. The difference
between "The New Deal" and the "Green New Deal"
starts in its creation. There weren't lobbying groups or
social media trends influencing legislation around
"The New Deal". Young people weren't crowding the
halls of the capitol buildings demanding social security. Much of the components of "The New Deal" were
hashed out between politicians behind closed doors.
The Green New Deal was created by activists and lob-
byist groups. It was carried by politicians. The activist
sphere essentially coordinated a power grab by writing
and attempting to pass legislation. Why didn't politicians just do what they did the first time and write this
proposal themselves? The answer is simple, it's because
The Great Depression and the existential threat of

climate change are addressed in two different stages. By the time of the creation of The New Deal, millions of Americans were already unemployed and standing in bread lines. The financial system had already crashed and the rest of the world was feeling it. America had to act. The crisis was happening in real time and the consequences couldn't be ignored or delayed. The climate crisis is different. Yes, there are parts of our country and world that are already feeling the effects of global warming and other human induced climate blunders, but it hasn't truly been felt or fully recognized by the masses. Activists are being proactive in their solution, which is what this country wasn't blessed with before the Great Depression. Had there been a solution to regulate the markets before they crashed, then the calamities that followed the Great Depression wouldn't have occurred. Many historians attribute the rise of Adolph Hitler to the market crash in the United States. What many of climate change's staunchest opposers don't foresee is the unintended domino effect of negative consequences that will follow. Cities will fall and oceans will rise. Democracies will fall and dictatorships will rise. Life will fall and death will rise. This power grab by activists should be viewed through the lens of passengers on a ship overriding the will of the Captain because he or she refuses to steer clear of icebergs. In the 30s, the Democrats had a trifecta and that helped tremendously, but one must also remember that this was when conservative Democrats also had a noticeable presence in the party. The main point is that the citizenry is stepping up and trying to do something before it's too late. This understanding put me in a tough situation. I felt as if I had to choose. Was I going to side with the activist sphere or was I going to side with the political sphere? I felt like no matter which option I opted for, I would end up disappointing a significant amount of people. I knew that I wanted to make an impact, and that politics offered me a route to go down. Though my initial exposure to politics through the MN Green New Deal dealt more with the political side of things; the genuine connections I made were all created in the activist sphere. I knew that many had to make similar decisions before me, and that many would make similar decisions after me. Not being able to communicate with anyone in either camp without also receiving a sizable amount of bias made the whole decision-making process feel so isolating. In the first stage of my decision making, I concluded that both sides had benefits. As a politician, you're in the room. You have a vote. Everywhere you go, you are no longer only carrying yourself, you're carrying your entire constituency — however many people that may be. As an activist, you speak your truth. You are unbeholden to anything but your values. You can put as much pressure on the system as you want. I know that my organizing going forward will involve a mixture of both.

Chapter 6:

Trouble In Paradise

A call to leadership.

A QUARTER THROUGH MY SENIOR year, news of a new disease overseas broke. I didn't think much of it at the time. I remember attending a political rally and sitting next to someone with a full-blown gas mask. I found it comical that someone would go to that length to protect themselves from a virus that was virtually nonexistent. The idea of covering one's face in public for any reason was foreign to me. Within what seemed like a week of the first reported case in the United States, in-person school instruction was out for the remainder of the year. COVID-19 was here, and we weren't ready. I went through the last day of my senior year without knowing it. The amount of uncertainty that rocked our country will be remembered for generations. Hundreds of thousands dead. Millions ended up getting severely sick. I remember feeling a sense of sadness and pity for my mother. Luckily, my sister and I were old enough to take care of ourselves, but I couldn't imagine how it must have felt to take on the economic uncertainty as a single parent. Our family's small business took a hit, but it was able to recover. The sudden end to our school year taught me one of the most valuable lessons in life: expect the unexpected. I remember engaging in an argument with a couple of students in my class through a mass virtual group containing all the students in our graduating class. The student leadership was trying to plan an autonomous social event in case school didn't resume; which, in my opinion, was one of the dumbest things I've read to date. The idea that in the beginning of a mysterious pandemic (with local cases), people would want to congregate simply to have fun was dangerous and selfish. No one knew the full effects and immunity surrounding the disease. The once foreign idea of covering one's face became an everyday reality for me. My family was glued to the television set, and we felt helpless watching the series of apocalyptic events unfold. The greatest source of my fear wasn't the possibility of catching COVID-19, it was the instability of our leadership at the top. President Trump set the bar to a new low by ignoring the protocols that had been put in place by the previous administration during the Ebola outbreak in Sierra Leone. The only reason I would tune in to the daily shenanigan press briefings was to listen to what Dr. Fauci had to say. It was during this time period that I saw what I believe to be one of the most selfless political moves in my lifetime. The Democratic primary was in full force before the pandemic hit our shores. Bernie Sanders was running the strongest grassroots campaign in American history. The galvanization that arose from his consistency and compassion paid off with three straight victories out of the first four contests. He had the organization to win and the ideas to transform this country towards a fundamentally new direction. When the pandemic hit, the primary was just heating up due to an unexpected strong showing from Joe

Biden during the first Super Tuesday. As more people were getting sick, the pandemic became the number one issue on every political campaign. COVID-19 altered how we interacted profoundly. Instead of continuing the primary, Bernie put his presidential ambitions aside for the common good of both his supporters and his opponent's supporters. This move alone cost Bernie the primary, but saved thousands of lives. Politics aside, the grim milestones that were being met in relation to the infection rate and death toll were emotionally tough to stomach. Several months into the pandemic, the daily apocalyptic narratives became the new norm. I remember shopping at Target on Lake Street when my sister gave me a call. I answered, assuming she was just curious about my whereabouts. Instead of asking me where I was, she asked me if I saw the video. "What video?" I replied. She told me about a fresh video that had been circulating around the internet of a black man being killed by police. The Black Lives Matter movement started back in 2013 with the acquittal of George Zimmerman — the murderer of Trayvon Martin. Although I was disappointed and infuriated by a senseless murder, I wasn't terribly surprised. I asked for the details. I paused when she said it happened in our city (Minneapolis) and I couldn't believe her description of the murder. George Floyd wasn't shot. He was suffocated by an officer's knee. I told her to save it until I got him and hung up. Before I put my phone back in my pocket, I noticed some unread notifications from neighbors planning a way to head to the protest slated for later that evening. It was at this moment that I started to grasp how urgent and explosive this situation was going to be. I felt the energy that this time was different. I rushed home and turned on the Television to see a man screaming for his mother, pleading for mercy, turning purple in the face. For over nine minutes, I watched a man's life leave his body in agony. Civilians pleading and admonishing police officers to let him breathe. I remember feeling a sense of hollowness after learning about the death of Michael Brown in Ferguson, then learning about the death of Eric Garner in New York City, then Freddie Gray, Sandra Bland, Jamaar Clark, Philando Castile, the list goes on. This time was different. It looked like a public execution. There was no denying who was in the wrong. There was no room for excuses from the police force or Republicans. Derek Chauvin's

knee on George Floyd's neck while the other officers
stood by and watched, finally showcased to the world
what a segment of American society already knew.
Because of that video, Black Lives Matter became the
largest political movement in American history. After
watching it several times, I grew more and more out-
raged by the utter lack of remorse for human life. I
texted a couple of my neighbors and attended what
was a huge peaceful demonstration on 38th &
Chicago. After an hour of standing, there was talk of
a march towards Lake Street where the Third Precinct
was located. The officers who murdered George Floyd
worked at the third precinct, so it only seemed right
to hold space there, too. Hundreds began to march
towards the Third Precinct and I joined a legion of
maybe forty people led by a passionate woman with a
bull horn. We took the long way and ended up getting
to the precinct later than the larger hoard. When we
got there, all hell had broken loose. Thousands had
occupied the small intersection in front of the Third
Precinct and the air was filled with tear gas. Officers
were standing on top of the precinct, indiscriminately
shooting rubber bullets and tear gas canisters at people on the ground. What made the situation worse was

the presence of young children, elders, and people with disabilities. As the demonstration turned into a stand off, the number of protesters grew. I managed to keep a safe distance from the standoff that night, but soaking it in from a distance was traumatizing. The Third Precinct was two minutes away from my house and two minutes away from my high school. The familiar route that I'd driven down for years suddenly looked and felt different. It was as if the infrastructure that made up the building that held the Third precinct became the manifestation of police brutality. Never had I seen a reaction so explosive and persistent. I could only compare it to a bee hive rejecting its queen bee. The strange thing about the timing of the murder of George Floyd on a personal level for me was the conversation that our family had two days before his murder. My uncle randomly shared a memory from 1992 after the beating of Rodney King and the unrest that followed. I remember thinking to myself, I wonder if a recorded instance of police brutality could spark a similar series of events today. Baltimore and Ferguson were the locations of two notable isolated cases of unrest in response to police brutality. I didn't think that what happened in 1992 could repeat itself. I was wrong. Twenty-eight years later, history repeated itself. This time, it was worse. The problem had been brewing up for decades and the American people reached their melting point. Realization and reflection were the two methods of thought that I left with on the first night of demonstrations. Was this the end of police brutality, or was this the end of America? I concluded that only time would tell. The next day, my entire family was glued to our television set. Our city was making international headlines. The Minneapolis Police Department released an insensitive statement calling for patience. The department went as far as to say that they believed Floyd's death was caused by a natural medical incident. This infuriated the country even more. As the crowds grew, the Minneapolis Police Department grew weaker in their ability to contain the anger across the city. I remember going home one night after demonstrating and being called into the living room to see Lake Street burning. The images of Lake Street burning meant that the level of anger and unrest was entering a new stage. The next day, Minnesotans from all across the state came out in the thousands to help restore parts of Minneapolis. The next night of demonstrations grew louder and stronger. Demonstrations spread from sea to shining sea. In situations like these, there tends to be a reactionary response to the mass acts of looting and rioting. I'm not condoning these types of acts, but I prefer to analyze the entirety of the situation. There's a reason why looting and rioting do not occur on a daily basis. The social fabric of our society prevents it through accountability. That accountability isn't only provided by law enforcement. The citizenry also bands together to support and maintain order in their community. Ideally, a partnership would be built between communities and law enforcement fostered through trust and solidarity. It takes both sides to maintain optimal calm and safety. When one side fails to carry out their end of the bargain, then the social contract is breached; in other words, all hell breaks loose. That's not to say that immediately addressing social upheaval is wrong. However, we mustn't let that aspect consume the entire narrative. Addressing its cause isn't only a preventative step, it's a necessary one to address the current problem. The problem shouldn't become less visible or pertinent as soon as people go home. Although I didn't appreciate a lot of the narrative forming that was happening, I appreciated one of the new narratives forming about Black Lives Matter. Critics could no longer dismiss it as divisive or singular because of the demographic of people who continuously showed up nationwide. I believe that the diversity of protestors, mainly in age and race, changed the national mood towards systemic racism and the Black Lives Matter movement. Martin Luther King Jr. was a constant figure who came up in discussion regarding which tactics were most effective. Although Dr. King championed the non-violent route; he didn't completely snuff what he called "righteous anger." He once called riots the "language of the unheard." I feel like that was Dr. King's way of saying that although he could not publicly stand behind it, he understood it. The images coming out of Minneapolis set off cities across the country. The National Guard was deployed in fifteen states in an effort to quell the unrest. Of all the nights of unrest in Minneapolis, there was one night that stood out the most. Demonstrators gathered on Lake Street as they had been doing for the past several nights; I stayed at home that night due to burnout. As I watched a live stream of what I believed to be an unusually large crowd gathered, I felt a peculiar

energy that I hadn't felt on any of the other nights.
Because of the influx of people, it was hard to see
exactly what was going on. It became clear that the
combination of a trigger-hyper mini police force outnumbered at least fifty to one against the disillusioned
and unforgiving crowd of thousands wasn't going to
end peacefully. The camera angle I was viewing cut to
an area behind the 3rd Precinct where dozens of cop
cars were preceded by a phalanx of police officers. The
intentions of the mobilization were unknown in the
beginning, but as the mobilization grew increasingly
unresponsive, a retreat was imminent. I don't think
anyone on either side of the precinct thought that a
retreat was even possible. The abandonment of the
3rd Precinct ushered in a dawn in both the protests in
response to the murder of George Floyd, and the overall struggle for racial justice in America.
Demonstrators took control of the 3rd Precinct and
burnt a significant portion of it down to the ground.
One didn't need to be in support of the burning to
recognize the significance of the 3rd Precinct's fall.
The Mayor attempted to cover the overpowering of
the police department by stating that he ordered officers to flee, but it was clear by the footage leading up

to the retreat, it was never an option for the officers or
the mayor to make. Thousands who weren't expected
to show up showed up, and this was the end result.
The next day a poll came out showing that the majority of Americans felt that the burning of the 3rd
Precinct was justified. From that moment on, officers
from the 3rd Precinct were nowhere to be seen. The
issue that once seemingly only negatively impacting
one demographic of Americans was now the number
one issue for all. It was no longer ignorable. The Trump
administration saw a country divided and sought to
divide it even further. Through insensitive comments
and National Guard deployments, the President of the
United States showcased a level of ineptitude our
country hadn't seen in decades. The officers who were
responsible for the murder of George Floyd were ter-
minated, then subsequently charged. The protests
continued as the seasons changed, and there was a
palpable tension that could be felt looming over
Minneapolis leading up to the trial. During the trial,
a young man named Daunte Wright was murdered by
a police officer in Brooklyn Center, Minnesota. The
video showed a police officer by the name of Kim
Potter deploying her hand gun and shooting Daunte

Wright at close range. Kim repeatedly shouted Taser in the video, but it's hard to believe that she mistook her Taser for a gun due to her extensive Taser training, and the instantly noticeable color, weight, location, and shape of a Taser compared to a gun. Although Brooklyn Center was nearly thirty minutes away from my house, I felt an obligation to be on the ground with Daunte Wright's family and demonstrators. The protests in Brooklyn Center received national attention as the timing of Daunte Wright's murder was synonymous with both the murder of George Floyd and the trial of Derek Chauvin. Hundreds gathered across the street from the Brooklyn Center police department building as the nights grew colder.

On one of the nights, I found myself positioned next to a CNN crew. A reporter named Sarah Snider asked if I wanted to be interviewed. I accepted Sarah's offer, understanding the reach of CNN and the opportunity to send a deeper message to the residents of Brooklyn Center. While thinking about the potential reach of my comments thirty seconds prior to my interview, I got a flashback to the beginning of the George Floyd protests at a press conference that

Donald Trump held. President Trump made a bizarre claim that demonstrators were hurling soup cans at law enforcement. He talked about the supposed logistics behind why it may be more auspicious to throw soup cans over other heavier projectiles. I felt that displaying a soup can in my interview would showcase both the memory and cleverness of organizers and activists across the country. Clowning the former president was also my objective. The formation of my plan was extemporaneous. As Sarah began my live interview, I answered many of the questions in a normal manner, and then I found an opening to sneak in my "Soup for my family" comment. I originally didn't think much of my comment. I thought it may make a few people smile and maybe reach the desks of a few politicians, but the reaction to my comment was mind blowing. About thirty minutes after I got home from protesting that night, I received numerous text messages with links and congrats from people I know. Apparently, someone had taken a short clip of my interview (Soup for my family portion) and distributed it throughout the web. The video was spreading faster than a wildfire and I became an overnight sensation. The clip would continue to circulate for the next couple of days, and the phone calls continued to come in. Perhaps the proudest thing about this event was the boom in attention — not for me — but for Daunte Wright. Overnight, the national awareness of his senseless killing had risen. The proof was in the number of demonstrators that turned out the next night, and the night after that. This series of events not only highlighted the importance of symbolism and messaging, but it also highlighted how powerful of an impact a moral boost can have on mobilization efforts. On April 20th, several months after the murder of George Floyd. The jury found Derek Chauvin guilty on all three counts of murder. I was filled with mixed emotions after the reading of the verdict. A part of me was relieved that the proper verdict was given. Derek Chauvin was guilty, and there was no doubt about it. Another part of me was somber. The idea that George Floyd wouldn't get to see his legacy play out, or his daughter graduate, haunted me. True justice would have been bringing George Floyd back. In the end, the ruling was one small step for justice, one giant leap for accountability. I believe that one of the most effective ways of solving a large issue is by taking it on bit by bit in unison. That's why in December 2020, I capitalized on the energy in the streets to better my community. The neighborhood group that I'd been Vice President of wasn't reflective of the will of the community. It was extremely difficult to propose or pass progressive ideas. It felt like my elevation to the position was done in an effort to tokenize my identity, or worst, atone feelings of guilt. I refused to allow the imprisonment of my potential. If I was going to carry out an agenda; it was going to be the people's agenda. I rallied several neighbors to run in elections, hoping to create a slate of like-minded progressives committed to representing the will of the neighborhood. Though it was difficult at first, the right people emerged and the slate was created. I made the decision to keep the slate of candidates private for strategic reasons. In due time, these candidates would present themselves to the public. Our neighborhood group elections were held online due to coronavirus concerns. Although I had a deep yearning to return to in-person gatherings, I must admit that I was actually quite relieved that this election would take place virtually. It spared me a lot of awkwardness. The expectation amongst board members was that I would fill the retiring board seats with progressive candidates, giving me some, but not too much, sway over agendas. I had a different plan, though. My plan was to go big or go home. I would contest every seat in the hopes of gaining a majority. My seat wasn't up for election until the following year. I chose to contest every seat, understanding the risk in the event that the slate of progressive candidates was defeated. I went for broke because of the sense of urgency surrounding the murder of George Floyd. The neighborhoods closest to the site needed to be the first to lead in change. For once in its history, our neighborhood group could actually represent not only the will, but the demographics of the neighborhood as a whole. We were determined to walk the talk, and we did. When the facilitator of the election asked for any floor nominations, that's when we struck. The entire slate announced their intentions and every seat except for mine was contested. I also decided to deploy my endorsement list, which played a pivotal role in our group's victory. The list caused an uproar amongst incumbent board members who were caught off guard. Several board members expressed their dismay to me privately after the votes had been cast. A couple of days later, as the results were released, it had become clear how large of a mandate we were given by the community. We won every seat by a landslide. As the result of one election, progressives had locally taken over the steering wheel. I faced what at the time felt like a profuse amount of anger, but also, at the same time, an equally felt outpouring of support. The one thing I didn't anticipate was the immoral limits some of the angered folks were willing to go to not only sabotage our agenda, but the overall reputation of the neighborhood group. The moment the results were posted, there were already well-connected forces advancing their obstruction. They adopted an 'if I can't have it, neither can you' mentality. That's when I learned that the real work doesn't stop after election day; the real work begins after election day. The first hurdle I faced was with our executive director. Several former board members who lost met with her and pledged their support for the organization so long as they didn't have to work in proximity to me. This was an issue in the eyes of our executive director because she was extremely new. She didn't want to lose support from neighbors, regardless of ideological beliefs. I met with her and informed her of my plans to run for president of the organization, unaware of the conversations she'd had with outgoing board members. In my mind, I was the only viable candidate. I was the most senior board member, and I had the full support of the new board. Once told of my plans, she cringed and responded with, "I don't know." It came as a shock. I was the deciding vote on her nomination as executive director a couple of months back. The conservative board members who'd sought to block her nomination were now influencing her feelings towards me. The meeting took a turn and things ended on an awkwardly standoffish basis. Our executive director then utilized her connection with some of the newer board members to express her reservations about my inevitable nomination for president. This created a rift that only grew until the final days of my presidency. Ultimately, as the new board was ushered, elections took place for officer roles and I was unanimously elected to the presidency. I spent a lot of time lobbying a small portion of new board members due to doubts that had arisen from our executive director's perturbations. In the end, I was able to convince that small contingency to support my bid based on my experience and based on the show of unity that would be needed to overcome the old guard's future attempts at obstruction. Little did I know, this hurdle was the first of many. As committee chairmanships changed and as previous policies were reformed, the old guard grew angrier and impatient. Within the group of new board members, factions started to form, only making the internal tension worse. Eventually, things reached a point of no return and our executive director chose to resign. During one of our monthly meetings, everything came full circle when two newly elected board members crafted a motion to remove me and the vice president from our respective positions. This move was unexpected and unforgivable. Actions for removal must be deliberately discussed and thought through before proposed. In one night, a couple of board members decided that they would attempt to sneak attack leadership. This was a form of public humiliation. A vote was called and the motion to remove us failed. This show of division was all the old guard needed to succeed in their plan of obstruction. As the in-fighting continued throughout the months, board members began to resign and the board eventually fell below the minimum mandate for a quorum. The mass resignations triggered a special election, which was then followed by a sweep of old guard candidates. The old guard was able to pick up every open seat and regain a majority on the board. At this point, I'd been seriously considering resigning from my seat, as it became clear that my brand of leadership wasn't going to fare well with the new makeup of the board. In all honesty, I'd been considering resigning months earlier as the in-fighting began to reach new lows. Being the youngest neighborhood group president, let alone board member, came with its fair share of challenges. It wasn't until after my presidency through reflection that I understood that many of the reactions I got from folks were based on my age. Some people simply couldn't take instructions from, or sincerely listen to, someone their grandkid's age. Some mid-aged professionals were too ambitious or impatient to understand why I had achieved more than them with only half the time on earth. I figured I'd see what the plans were of the new majority and decide whether it would be a good match. After the election, I met with a majority of the new members to congratulate them on their victories and to gage what their collective vision was for the organization — that's right, they also ran as a slate. Surprisingly enough, the sentiment from the majority wasn't to have me removed. They recognized the important institutional knowledge I brought to the table and asked me to stay on the board. I figured I'd be able to compromise in several areas to accomplish meaningful work for the community. A month after the election of the new board, it seemed like there was an agreement in place. My analysis was wrong. During a regularly scheduled private executive committee meeting, one of the old guard members asked to add a motion and I agreed to the motion, assuming it was to wish another old guard member a happy birthday. The old guard member proceeded to read a three-page document that accused the vice-president and me of pretty much everything wrong under the sun. This document was used as a threat. The board member gave me an ultimatum. If I resigned, the document would magically disappear. If I chose to fight it out, then the document would be shown to the public tarnishing my reputation. 99% of the document was false. It was extremely messy and hard to fully comprehend. Had this happened several months ago, I would have rallied dozens of neighbors after sounding the drums of war. This time was different. Maybe it was burnout from battles past, or maybe it was the acknowledgement that this battle wouldn't be won. I chose to resign not out of fear, but out of responsibility. The neighborhood group suffered tremendously over the past several months due to internal and external conflict. The standing of the organization was in question, and the short and long-term goals set in place were compromised. If I engaged in this conflict, I would survive, but the neighborhood group wouldn't. Once a leader is motivated by spite or revenge, then those principles become the motivation to remove them. I had my moment in the sun, and it was time to go inside. The remaining allied board members of mine resigned in solidarity once again, putting the organization below the minimum mandate of board members. I chose to title the final chapter of my book "Trouble In Paradise" because the time period between 2016 to 2021 has shown to be just that. America has experienced a new kind of pressure. This pressure isn't being applied through an external force, but an internal force. The exacerbation of our problems can be traced back to a lack of leadership. Our democratic systems are eroding and national unity has become a mirage. Our generation has prematurely been placed on the vanguard in terms of holding elected officials accountable mainly through protests. This thrust is analogous to shoving an unexpecting individual off a diving board into a twenty foot pool. As our American Mosaic continues to expand, one may question whether the canvass is large enough to contain our masterpiece. Recent rhetoric shows that one canvass isn't enough, and that two or three separate canvases will suffice. I disagree. I believe that we have, and always will, be one great mosaic with a level of diversity that is inconceivable to the human eye. Regardless of how history portrays our collective story, here's my story. Our narrative won't be singular, but plural. As I look into the eyes of every man, woman, and child, I see pieces of our collective story. I see our Mosaic Republic.